# ESSAYS
## ON
## SUICIDE
## AND
## THE IMMORTALITY
### OF THE
## SOUL,

BY THE LATE

*DAVID HUME*, Esq.

With REMARKS by the EDITOR.

TO WHICH ARE ADDED,

TWO LETTERS ON SUICIDE,

FROM ROSSEAU'S ELOISA.

═══════

A NEW EDITION,

WITH CONSIDERABLE IMPROVEMENTS.

───────

LONDON.

Printed for G. KEARSLEY; and sold by the Booksellers in
Piccadilly, Fleet-street, and Paternoster Row.

1789.

Price Four Shillings in Boards.

# PREFACE.

THESE two Essays on *Suicide* and *the Immortality of the Soul*, though not published in any edition of his works, are generally attributed to the late ingenious Mr. Hume.

The well-known contempt of this eminent philosopher for the common convictions of mankind, raised an apprehension of the contents from the very title of these pieces. But the celebrity of the author's name renders them, notwithstanding, in some degree, objects of great curiosity.

Owing to this circumstance, a few copies have been clandestinely circulated, at a large price, for some time, but without any comment. The very mystery attending this mode of selling them, made them more an object of request than they would otherwise have been.

The present publication comes abroad under no such restraint, and possesses very superior advantages. The *Notes* annexed are intended to expose the sophistry contained in the original Essays, and may shew how little we have to fear from the adversaries of these great truths, from the pitiful figure

figure which even Mr. Hume makes in thus violently exhausting his last strength in an abortive attempt to traduce or discredit them.

The two very masterly Letters from the Eloisa of Rosseau on the subject of *Suicide*, have been much celebrated, and we hope will be considered as materially increasing the value of this curious collection.

The admirers of *Mr. Hume* will be pleased with seeing the remains of a favorite author rescued in this manner from that oblivion to which the prejudices of his countrymen had, in all appearance, consigned them; and even the religious part of mankind have some reason of triumph from the striking instance here given of truth's superiority to error, even when error has all the advantage of an elegant genius, and a great literary reputation to recommend it.

M.

# ESSAY I.

## On SUICIDE.

ONE confiderable advantage that arifes from Philofophy, confifts in the fovereign antidote which it affords to fuperftition or falfe religion. All other remedies againft that peftilent diftemper are vain, or at leaft uncertain. Plain good fenfe and the practice of the world, which alone ferve moft purpofes of life, are here found ineffectual: Hiftory as well as daily experience furnifh inftances of men endowed with the ftrongeft strongest capacity for business and affairs, who have all their lives crouched under slavery to the grossest superstition. Even gaiety and sweetness of temper, which infuse a balm into every other wound, afford no remedy to so virulent a poison; as we may particularly observe of the fair sex, who tho' commonly possest of these rich presents of nature, feel many of their joys blasted by this importunate intruder. But when sound Philosophy has once gained possession of the mind, superstition is effectually excluded, and one may fairly affirm that her triumph over this enemy is more complete than over most of the vices and imperfections incident to human nature. Love or anger, ambition or avarice, has its root in the temper and affections, which the soundest reason is scarce ever able fully to correct; but superstition being founded on false opinion, must immediately vanish when true philosophy has inspired juster sentiments of superior powers. The contest is here more equal between the distemper and the medicine, and nothing can hinder the latter

from

from proving effectual but its being false and sophisticated.

It will here be superfluous to magnify the merits of Philosophy by displaying the pernicious tendency of that vice of which it cures the human mind. (1) The superstitious man, says Tully *, is miserable in every scene, in every incident of life; even sleep itself, which banishes all other cares of unhappy mortals, affords to him matter of new terror; while he examines his dreams, and finds in those visions of the night prognostications of future calamities. I may add that tho' death alone can put a full period to his misery, he dares not fly to this refuge, but still prolongs a miserable existence from a vain fear lest he offend his Maker, by using the power, with which that beneficent Being has endowed him. The presents of God and nature are ravished from us by this cruel enemy, and notwithstanding that one step would remove us from the regions of pain and sorrow, her menaces still chain us down

* De Divin. lib. ii.

down to a hated being which she herself chiefly contributes to render miserable.

'Tis observed by such as have been reduced by the calamities of life to the necessity of employing this fatal remedy, that if the unseasonable care of their friends deprive them of that species of Death which they proposed to themselves, they seldom venture upon any other, or can summon up so much resolution a second time as to execute their purpose. So great is our horror of death, that when it presents itself under any form, besides that to which a man has endeavoured to reconcile his imagination, it acquires new terrors, and overcomes his feeble courage: But when the menaces of superstition are joined to this natural timidity, no wonder it quite deprives men of all power over their lives, since even many pleasures and enjoyments, to which we are carried by a strong propensity, are torn from us by this inhuman tyrant. Let us here endeavour to restore men to their native liberty, by examining all the

the common arguments against Suicide, and shewing that that action may be free from every imputation of guilt or blame, according to the sentiments of all the ancient philosophers. (2)

If Suicide be criminal, it must be a transgression of our duty either to God, our neighbour, or ourselves.—To prove that suicide is no transgression of our duty to God, the following considerations may perhaps suffice. In order to govern the material world, the almighty Creator has established general and immutable laws, by which all bodies, from the greatest planet to the smallest particle of matter, are maintained in their proper sphere and function. To govern the animal world, he has endowed all living creatures with bodily and mental powers; with senses, passions, appetites, memory, and judgment, by which they are impelled or regulated in that course of life to which they are destined. These two distinct principles of the material and animal world, continually encroach upon each other, and mutually retard or forward each others operation. The powers of men and of all other animals are restrained and directed by the nature and qualities of the surrounding bodies; and the modifications and actions of these bodies are incessantly altered by the operation of all animals. Man is stopt by rivers in his passage over the surface of the earth; and rivers, when properly directed, lend their force to the motion of machines, which serve to the use of man. But though the provinces of the material and animal powers are not kept entirely separate, there results from thence no discord or disorder in the creation; on the contrary, from the mixture, union, and contrast of all the various powers of inanimate bodies and living creatures arise that sympathy, harmony, and proportion, which afford the surest argument of Supreme Wisdom. The providence of the Deity appears not immediately in any operation, but governs every thing by those general and immutable laws, which have been established from the beginning of time.

time. All events, in one sense, may be pronounced the action of the Almighty; they all proceed from those powers with which he has endowed his creatures. A house which falls by its own weight, is not brought to ruin by his providence, more than one destroyed by the hands of men; nor are the human faculties less his workmanship, than the laws of motion and gravitation. When the passions play, when the judgment dictates, when the limbs obey; this is all the operation of God, and upon these animate principles, as well as upon the inanimate, has he established the government of the universe. Every event is alike important in the eyes of that infinite Being, who takes in at one glance the most distant regions of space, and remotest periods of time. There is no event, however important to us, which he has exempted from the general laws that govern the universe, or which he has peculiarly reserved for his own immediate action and operation. The revolution of states and empires depends upon

the

the smallest caprice or passion of single men; and the lives of men are shortened or extended by the smallest accident of air or diet, sunshine or tempest. Nature still continues her progress and operation; and if general laws be ever broke by particular volitions of the Deity, 'tis after a manner which entirely escapes human observation. As, on the one hand, the elements and other inanimate parts of the creation carry on their action without regard to the particular interest and situation of men; so men are entrusted to their own judgment and discretion in the various shocks of matter, and may employ every faculty with which they are endowed, in order to provide for their ease, happiness, or preservation. What is the meaning then of that principle, that a man, who tired of life, and hunted by pain and misery, bravely overcomes all the natural terrors of death, and makes his escape from this cruel scene: that such a man, I say, has incurred the indignation of his Creator by encroaching on the office of Divine Providence, and disturbing the order of the universe? Shall we assert that the Almighty has reserved to himself in any peculiar manner the disposal of the lives of men, and has not submitted that event in common with others, to the general laws by which the universe is governed? This is plainly false; the lives of men depend upon the same laws as the lives of all other animals; and these are subjected to the general laws of matter and motion. The fall of a tower, or the infusion of a poison, will destroy a man equally with the meanest creature; an inundation sweeps away every thing, without distinction that comes within the reach of its fury. Since, therefore, the lives of men are for ever dependent on the general laws of matter and motion, is a man's disposing of his life criminal, because in every case it is criminal to encroach upon these laws, or disturb their operation? But this seems absurd; all animals are entrusted to their own prudence and skill for their conduct in the world, and have

full

full authority, as far as their power extends, to alter all the operations of nature. Without the exercise of this authority they could not subsist a moment; every action, every motion of a man, innovates on the order of some parts of matter, and diverts from their ordinary course the general laws of motion. Putting together, therefore, these conclusions, we find that human life depends upon the general laws of matter and motion, and that it is no encroachment on the office of providence to disturb or alter these general laws: Has not every one, of consequence, the free disposal of his own life? And may he not lawfully employ that power with which nature has endowed him? In order to destroy the evidence of this conclusion we must shew a reason why this particular case is excepted; is it because human life is of such great importance, that 'tis a presumption for human prudence to dispose of it? But the life of a man is of no greater importance to the universe than that of an oyster. And were it of ever so great importance

portance, the order of human nature has actually submitted it to human prudence, and reduced us to a necessity, in every incident, of determining concerning it.—Were the disposal of human life so much reserved as the peculiar province of the Almighty, that it were an encroachment on his right, for men to dispose of their own lives; it would be equally criminal to act for the preservation of life as for its destruction. If I turn aside a stone which is falling upon my head, I disturb the course of nature, and I invade the peculiar province of the Almighty, by lengthening out my life beyond the period which by the general laws of matter and motion he had assigned it. (3)

A hair, a fly, an insect is able to destroy this mighty being whose life is of such importance. Is it an absurdity to suppose that human prudence may lawfully dispose of what depends on such insignificant causes? It would be no crime in me to divert the *Nile* or *Danube* from its course,

were

were I able to effect such purposes. Where then is the crime of turning a few ounces of blood from their natural channel?—Do you imagine that I repine at Providence or curse my creation, because I go out of life, and put a period to a being, which, were it to continue, would render me miserable? Far be such sentiments from me; I am only convinced of a matter of fact, which you yourself acknowledge possible, that human life may be unhappy, and that my existence, if further prolonged, would become ineligible; but I thank Providence, both for the good which I have already enjoyed, and for the power with which I am endowed of escaping the ill that threatens me.\* To you it belongs to repine at providence, who foolishly imagine that you have no such power, and who must still prolong a hated life, tho' loaded with pain and sickness, with shame and poverty.—— Do not you teach, that when any ill befals me, tho' by the malice of my enemies, I ought

\* Agamus Dei gratias, quod nemo in vita teneri potest.
Sen. Epist. 12

ought to be resigned to Providence, and that the actions of men are the operations of the Almighty as much as the actions of inanimate beings? When I fall upon my own sword, therefore, I receive my death equally from the hands of the Deity as if it had proceeded from a lion, a precipice, or a fever. The submission which you require to providence, in every calamity that befals me, excludes not human skill and industry, if possible by their means I can avoid or escape the calamity: And why may I not employ one remedy as well as another?—If my life be not my own, it were criminal for me to put it in danger, as well as to dispose of it; nor could one man deserve the appellation of *hero*, whom glory or friendship transports into the greatest dangers, and another merit the reproach of *wretch* or *miscreant* who puts a period to his life, from the same or like motives.—
—There is no being, which possesses any power or faculty, that it receives not from its Creator; nor is there any one, which by ever so irregular an action can encroach

upon

upon the plan of his providence, or disorder the universe. Its operations are his works equally with that chain of events which it invades; and which ever principle prevails, we may for that very reason conclude it to be most favoured by him. Be it animate or inanimate, rational or irrational, 'tis all a case: its power is still derived from the supreme Creator, and is alike comprehended in the order of his providence. When the horror of pain prevails over the love of life; when a voluntary action anticipates the effects of blind causes, 'tis only in consequence of those powers and principles which he has implanted in his creatures. Divine providence is still inviolate, and placed far beyond the reach of human injuries. 'Tis impious, says the old Roman superstition\*, to divert rivers from their course, or invade the prerogatives of nature: 'Tis impious, says the French superstition, to inoculate for the small-pox, or usurp the business of providence by voluntary producing distempers

\* Tacit. An. lib. i.

pers and maladies: 'Tis impious, says the modern *European* superstition, to put a period to our own life, and thereby rebel against our Creator; and why not impious, say I, to build houses, cultivate the ground, or sail upon the ocean? In all these actions we employ our powers of mind and body, to produce some innovation in the course of nature; and in none of them do we any more. They are all of them therefore equally innocent, or equally criminal. *But you are placed by Providence, like a sentinel, in a particular station, and when you desert it without being recalled, you are equally guilty of rebellion against your Almighty Sovereign, and have incurred his displeasure.*——I ask, why do you conclude that providence has placed me in this station? For my part I find that I owe my birth to a long chain of causes, of which many depended upon voluntary actions of men. *But providence guided all these causes, and nothing happens in the universe without its consent and co-operation.* If so, then neither does my death, however voluntary, happen without its con-

sent;

sent; and whenever pain or sorrow so far overcomes my patience, as to make me tired of life, I may conclude that I am recalled from my station in the clearest and most expressed terms. 'Tis providence surely that has placed me at this present in this chamber: But may I not leave it when I think proper, without being liable to the imputation of having deserted my post or station? When I shall be dead, the principles of which I am composed will still perform their part in the universe, and will be equally useful in the grand fabrick, as when they composed this individual creature. The difference to the whole will be no greater than betwixt my being in a chamber and in the open air. The one change is of more importance to me than the other; but not more so to the universe.

'Tis a kind of blasphemy to imagine that any created being can disturb the order of the world, or invade the business of Providence! it supposes, that that being

ing possesses powers and faculties, which it received not from its Creator, and which are not subordinate to his government and authority. A man may disturb society, no doubt, and thereby incur the displeasure of the Almighty. But the government of the world is placed far beyond his reach and violence. And how does it appear that the Almighty is displeased with those actions that disturb society? By the principles which he has implanted in human nature, and which inspire us with a sentiment of remorse if we ourselves have been guilty of such actions, and with that of blame and disapprobation, if we ever observe them in others:—Let us now examine, according to the method proposed, whether Suicide be of this kind of actions, and be a breach of our duty to our *neighbour* and to *society*.

A MAN who retires from life does no harm to society: He only ceases to do good; which, if it is an injury, is of the lowest kind.—All our obligations to do good

good to society seem to imply something reciprocal. I receive the benefits of society, and therefore ought to promote its interests; but when I withdraw myself altogether from society, can I be bound any longer? But allowing that our obligations to do good were perpetual, they have certainly some bounds; I am not obliged to do a small good to society at the expence of a great harm to myself; why then should I prolong a miserable existence, because of some frivolous advantage which the public may perhaps receive from me? If upon account of age and infirmities, I may lawfully resign any office, and employ my time altogether in fencing against these calamities, and alleviating, as much as possible, the miseries of my future life: Why may I not cut short these miseries at once by an action which is no more prejudicial to society?—But suppose that it is no longer in my power to promote the interest of society; suppose that I am a burden to it; suppose that my life hinders some person

son from being much more useful to society. In such cases, my resignation of life must not only be innocent, but laudable. And most people who lie under any temptation to abandon existence, are in some such situation: those who have health, or power, or authority, have commonly better reason to be in humour with the world. (4)

A MAN is engaged in a conspiracy for the public interest; is seized upon suspicion; is threatened with the rack; and knows from his own weakness that the secret will be extorted from him: Could such a one consult the public interest better than by putting a quick period to a miserable life? This was the case of the famous and brave *Strozi* of *Florence.*──── Again, suppose a malefactor is justly condemned to a shameful death, can any reason be imagined, why he may not anticipate his punishment, and save himself all the anguish of thinking on its dreadful approaches? He invades the business

business of providence, no more than the magistrate did, who ordered his execution; and his voluntary death is equally advantageous to society, by ridding it of a pernicious member.

That Suicide may often be consistent with interest and with our duty to ourselves, no one can question, who allows that age, sickness, or misfortune, may render life a burthen, and make it worse even than annihilation. I believe that no man ever threw away life, while it was worth keeping. For such is our natural horror of death, that small motives will never be able to reconcile us to it; and though perhaps the situation of a man's health or fortune did not seem to require this remedy, we may at least be assured that any one who, without apparent reason, has had recourse to it, was curst with such an incurable depravity or gloominess of temper as must poison all enjoyment, and render him equally miserable as if he had been loaded ed with the most grievous misfortunes.—If suicide be supposed a crime, 'tis only cowardice can impel us to it. If it be no crime, both prudence and courage should engage us to rid ourselves at once of existence, when it becomes a burthen. 'Tis the only way that we can then be useful to society, by setting an example, which if imitated, would preserve to every one his chance for happiness in life, and would effectually free him from all danger of misery\*.

\* It would be easy to prove that suicide is as lawful under the Christian dispensation as it was to the Heathens. There is not a single text of scripture which prohibits it. That great and infallible rule of faith and practice which must controul all philosophy and human reasoning, has left us in this particular to our natural liberty. Resignation to Providence is indeed recommended in scripture; but that implies only submission to ills that are unavoidable, not to such as may be remedied by prudence or courage. *Thou shall not kill*, is evidently meant to exclude only the killing of others, over whose life we have no authority. That this precept, like most of the scripture precepts, must be modified by reason and common sense, is plain from the practice of magistrates,

gistrates, who punish criminals capitally, notwithstanding the letter of the law. But were this commandment ever so express against suicide, it would now have no authority, for all the law of *Moses* is abolished, except so far as it is established by the law of nature. And we have already endeavoured to prove that suicide is not prohibited by that law. In all cases, Christians and Heathens are precisely upon the same footing; *Cato* and *Brutus*, *Arrea* and *Portia* acted heroically; those who now imitate their example ought to receive the same praises from posterity. The power of committing suicide is regarded by *Pliny* as an advantage which men possess even above the Deity himself. "Deus non sibi potest mortem conscisere si velit quod homini dedit optimum in tantis vitæ pœnis." Lib. II, cap. 7. (5)

# ESSAY II.

## ON THE
## IMMORTALITY of the SOUL.

BY the mere light of reason, it seems difficult to prove the *Immortality* of the *Soul*; the arguments for it are commonly derived either from *metaphysical* topics, or *moral* or *physical*. But in reality 'tis the Gospel, and the Gospel alone, that has brought *life and immortality to light*.

I. METAPHYSICAL topics suppose that the [...] immaterial, and that 'tis impo[...] thought to belong to a material sub[...]——(1) But just metaphysics teach us that the notion of substance

stance is wholly confused and imperfect, and that we have no other idea of any substance, than as an aggregate of particular qualities, inhering in an unknown something. Matter, therefore, and spirit, are at bottom equally unknown, and we cannot determine what qualities inhere in the one or in the other. (2) They likewise teach us that nothing can be decided *a priori* concerning any cause or effect, and that experience being the only source of our judgments of this nature, we cannot know from any other principle, whether matter, by its structure or arrangement, may not be the cause of thought. Abstract reasonings cannot decide any question of fact or existence.—But admitting a spiritual substance to be dispersed throughout the universe, like the etherial fire of the *Stoics*, and to be the only inherent subject of thought, we have reason to conclude from analogy that nature uses it after the manner she does the other substance, matter. She employs it as a kind of paste or clay;
modi-

modifies it into a variety of forms and existences; dissolves after a time each modification, and from its substance erects a new form. As the same material substance may successively compose the bodies of all animals, the same spiritual substance may compose their minds: Their consciousness, or that system of thought which they formed during life, may be continually dissolved by death. And nothing interests them in the new modification. The most positive assertors of the mortality of the soul, never denied the immortality of its substance. And that an immaterial substance, as well as a material, may lose its memory or consciousness, appears in part from experience, if the soul be immaterial.—Reasoning from the common course of nature, and without supposing any new interposition of the supreme cause, which ought always to be excluded from philosophy, what is incorruptible must also be ingenerable. The Soul therefore, if immortal, existed before our birth; and if the former existence no ways concerned us, neither will the latter.—Animals undoubtedly feel, think, love, hate, will, and even reason, though in a more imperfect manner than men; are their souls also immaterial and immortal? (3)

II. Let us now consider the moral arguments, chiefly those derived from the justice of God, which is supposed to be farther interested in the farther punishment of the vicious and reward of the virtuous.—But these arguments are grounded on the supposition that God has attributes beyond what he has exerted in this universe, with which alone we are acquainted. Whence do we infer the existence of these attributes?—'Tis very safe for us to affirm, that whatever we know the Deity to have actually done, is best; but 'tis very dangerous to affirm, that he must always do what to us seems best. In how many instances would this reasoning fail us with regard to the present world?—But if any purpose of nature be clear,

clear, we may affirm, that the whole scope and intention of man's creation, so far as we can judge by natural reason, is limited to the present life. With how weak a concern from the original inherent structure of the mind and passions, does he ever look farther? What comparison either for steadiness or efficacy, betwixt so floating an idea, and the most doubtful persuasion of any matter of fact that occurs in common life. There arise indeed in some minds some unaccountable terrors with regard to futurity; but these would quickly vanish were they not artificially fostered by precept and education. And those who foster them, what is their motive? only to gain a livelihood, and to acquire power and riches in this world. Their very zeal and industry therefore is an argument against them.

WHAT cruelty, what iniquity, what injustice in nature, to confine all our concern, as well as all our knowledge, to the present life, if there be another scene still waiting us, of infinitely greater consequence? Ought this barbarous deceit to be ascribed to a beneficent and wise Being?—Observe with what exact proportion the task to be performed and the performing powers are adjusted throughout all nature. If the reason of man gives him great superiority above other animals, his necessities are proportionably multiplied upon him; his whole time, his whole capacity, activity, courage, and passion, find sufficient employment in fencing against the miseries of his present condition, and frequently, nay almost always are too slender for the business assigned them.—A pair of shoes perhaps was never yet wrought to the highest degree of perfection which that commodity is capable of attaining. Yet it is necessary, at least very useful, that there should be some politicians and moralists, even some geometers, poets, and philosophers among mankind. The powers of men are no more superior to their wants, considered

merely

merely in this life, than those of foxes and hares are, compared to *their* wants and to their period of existence. The inference from parity of reason is therefore obvious.

On the theory of the Soul's mortality, the inferiority of women's capacity is easily accounted for. Their domestic life requires no higher faculties, either of mind or body. This circumstance vanishes and becomes absolutely insignificant, on the religious theory: the one sex has an equal task to perform as the other; their powers of reason and resolution ought also to have been equal, and both of them infinitely greater than at present. As every effect implies a cause, and that another, till we reach the first cause of all, which is the Deity; every thing that happens is ordained by him, and nothing can be the object of his punishment or vengeance. —By what rule are punishments and rewards distributed? What is the divine standard of merit and demerit? Shall we suppose that human sentiments have place in the Deity? How bold that hypothesis! We have no conception of any other sentiments.—According to human sentiments, sense, courage, good manners, industry, prudence, genius, &c. &c. are essential parts of personal merits. Shall we therefore erect an elysium for poets and heroes like that of the ancient mythology? Why confine all rewards to one species of virtue? Punishment, without any proper end or purpose, is inconsistent with *our* ideas of goodness and justice, and no end can be served by it after the whole scene is closed. Punishment, according to *our* conception, should bear some proportion to the offence. Why then eternal punishment for the temporary offences of so frail a creature as man? Can any one approve of *Alexander*'s rage, who intended to exterminate a whole nation because they had seized his favourite horse Bucephalus? \*

HEAVEN

---

\* Quint. Curtius, lib. VI. cap. 5.

Heaven and Hell suppose two distinct species of men, the good and the bad; but the greatest part of mankind floats betwixt vice and virtue.—Were one to go round the world with an intention of giving a good supper to the righteous, and a sound drubbing to the wicked, he would frequently be embarrassed in his choice, and would find that the merits and the demerits of most men and women scarcely amount to the value of either.—To suppose measures of approbation and blame different from the human confounds every thing. Whence do we learn that there is such a thing as moral distinctions, but from our own sentiments?— What man who has not met with personal provocation (or what good-natured man who has) could inflict on crimes, from the sense of blame alone, even the common, legal, frivolous punishments? And does any thing steel the breast of judges and juries against the sentiments of humanity but reflection on necessity and public interest? By the Roman law

those

those who had been guilty of parricide, and confessed their crime, were put into a sack along with an ape, a dog, and a serpent, and thrown into the river. Death alone was the punishment of those who denied their guilt, however fully proved. A criminal was tried before *Augustus*, and condemned after a full conviction; but the humane emperor, when he put the last interrogatory, gave it such a turn as to lead the wretch into a denial of his guilt. " You surely (said the prince) did not kill your father."* This lenity suits our natural ideas of *right* even towards the greatest of all criminals, and even though it prevents so inconsiderable a sufferance. Nay even the most bigotted priest would naturally, without reflection, approve of it provided the crime was not heresy or infidelity; for as these crimes hurt himself in his *temporal* interest and advantages, perhaps he may not be

---

* Suet. August. cap. 3.

be altogether so indulgent to them. The chief source of moral ideas is the reflection on the interest of human society. Ought these interests, so short, so frivolous, to be guarded by punishments eternal and infinite? The damnation of one man is an infinitely greater evil in the universe, than the subversion of a thousand millions of kingdoms. Nature has rendered human infancy peculiarly frail and mortal, as it were on purpose to refute the notion of a probationary state; the half of mankind die before they are rational creatures.

III. The *Physical* arguments from the analogy of nature are strong for the mortality of the soul, and are really the only philosophical arguments which ought to be admitted with regard to this question, or indeed any question of fact.—Where any two objects are so closely connected that all alterations which we have ever seen in the one, or attended with proportionable alterations in the other, we

ought

ought to conclude, by all rules of analogy, that when there are still greater alterations produced in the former, and it is totally diffolved, there follows a total diffolution of the latter.—Sleep, a very small effect on the body, is attended with a temporary extinction, at leaft a great confufion in the foul.—The weakneſs of the body and that of the mind in infancy are exactly proportioned, their vigour in manhood, their fympathetic diforder in fickneſs; their common gradual decay in old age. The ſtep further ſeems unavoidable; their common diffolution in death. The laft fymptoms which the mind difcovers are diforder, weakneſs, infenſibility, and ftupidity, the forerunners of its annihilation. The farther progreſs of the ſame cauſes encreaſing, the ſame effects totally extinguiſh it. Judging by the uſual analogy of nature, no form can continue when transferred to a condition of life very different from the original one, in which it was placed. Trees periſh in the water, fiſhes in the air, animals

mals in the earth. Even so small a difference as that of climate is often fatal. What reason then to imagine, that an immense alteration, such as is made on the soul by the dissolution of its body, and all its organs of thought and sensation, can be effected without the dissolution of the whole? Every thing is in common betwixt soul and body. The organs of the one are all of them the organs of the other. The existence therefore of the one must be dependant on that of the other.—The souls of animals are allowed to be mortal; and these bear so near a resemblance to the souls of men, that the analogy from one to the other forms a very strong argument. Their bodies are not more resembling; yet no one rejects the argument drawn from comparative anatomy. The *Metempsychosis* is therefore the only system of this kind that philosophy can hearken to. (4)

NOTHING in this world is perpetual, every thing however seemingly firm is in con-

continual flux and change, the world itself gives symptoms of frailty and diffolution. How contrary to analogy, therefore, to imagine that one fingle form, feemingly the fraileft of any, and fubject to the greateft diforders, is immortal and indiffoluble? (5) What daring theory is that! how lightly, not to fay how rafhly entertained! How to difpofe of the infinite number of pofthumous exiftences ought alfo to embarrafs the religious theory. Every planet in every folar fyftem we are at liberty to imagine peopled with intelligent mortal beings, at leaft we can fix on no other fuppofition. For thefe then a new univerfe muft every generation be created beyond the bounds of the prefent univerfe, or one muft have been created at firft fo prodigioufly wide as to admit of this continual influx of beings. (6) Ought fuch bold fuppofitions to be received by any philofophy, and that merely on the pretext of a bare poffibility? When it is afked whether *Agamemnon, Therfites, Hannibal, Varro,* and
every

every stupid clown that ever exifted in *Italy, Scythia, Bactria* or *Guinea,* are now alive; can any man think, that a fcrutiny of nature will furnifh arguments ftrong enough to anfwer fo ftrange a queftion in the affirmative? The want of argument without revelation fufficiently eftablifhes the negative.—" *Quanto facilius* (fays *Pliny* \*) " *certius que fibi quemque credere, ac fpecimen fecuritatis antigene tali* " *fumere experimento.*" Our infenfibility before the compofition of the body feems to natural reafon a proof of a like ftate after diffolution.—Were our horrors of annihilation an original paffion, not the effect of our general love of happinefs, it would rather prove the mortality of the foul. For as nature does nothing in vain, fhe would never give us a horror againft an impoffible event. She may give us a horror againft an unavoidable event, provided our endeavours, as in the prefent cafe, may often remove it to fome diftance.

\* Lib. 7. cap. 55.

distance. Death is in the end unavoidable; yet the human species could not be preserved had not nature inspired us with an aversion towards it. All doctrines are to be suspected which are favoured by our passions; and the hopes and fears which gave rise to this doctrine are very obvious.

'Tis an infinite advantage in every controversy to defend the negative. If the question be out of the common experienced course of nature, this circumstance is almost if not altogether decisive. By what arguments or analogies can we prove any states of existence, which no one ever saw, and which no way resembles any that ever was seen? Who will repose such trust in any pretended philosophy as to admit upon its testimony the reality of so marvellous a scene? Some new species of logic is requisite for that purpose, and some new faculties of the mind, that may enable us to comprehend that logic.

NOTHING

NOTHING could set in a fuller light the infinite obligations which mankind have to divine revelation, since we find that no other medium could ascertain this great and important truth.

# ANTI-SUICIDE.

(1) THIS elaborate eulogium on philosophy points obliquely at religion, which we christians consider as the only sovereign antidote to every disease incident to the mind of man. It is indeed hard to say what reason might do were it freed from all restraints, especially if a succession of philosophers were incessantly improving on one another as they went on, avoiding and correcting the mistakes of those who preceded them in the same pursuit, till at last one complete and rational system was effected. Great things might probably be accomplished in this manner. But no such plan in fact ever was or is likely to be finished. Neither priestcraft, nor magisterial powers, however, cramped the progress of improving reason, or baffled the genius of enquiring man. The principles of religion and virtue were freely canvassed by the boldest spirits of antiquity. In truth, the superior advantage and necessity of the christian religion seems manifest from this particular circum-

circumstance, that it has taken away every possible restraint from natural religion, allowing it to exert itself to the utmost in finding out the fundamental truths of virtue, and in acquiescing in them, in openly avowing and acknowledging them when revealed, in extending the views and expectations of men, in giving them more just and liberal sentiments, and in publickly and uniformly disclaiming any intention of establishing a kingdom for its votaries or believers in this world.

The doctrines of the gospel are not intended to instruct us in the knowledge of every thing which may be really useful in the present life, far less of every thing, which, from curiosity alone, we may have a mighty desire to know. Revelation considers mankind in their highest capacity, as the rational and accountable subjects of God, and as capable both of present and future happiness or misery, according to their behaviour. Its chief if not its sole design, is to give us those views and impressions of our nature, of our state, of the perfections, the counsels, the laws, and the government of God, which, under the influence of providence, are the immediate and infallible means of the purity, of the comfort, and of the moral order, rectitude, and excellence of our immoral mortal souls. As corrupted and disordered, we are incapable of true happiness, till purified and restored to order. As guilty and mortal creatures, we can have no true consolation without the hopes of pardon in a future and separate state of existence. As surrounded with dangers, and obnoxious to every dismal apprehension, we can possess no solid or permanent content, but in the sincere and well grounded convictions of that gracious and righteous administration so minutely and explicity delineated in the scriptures. It is evident therefore that the principal excellence and utility of revealed truths must lie or consist in the influence they have upon the sanctification and consolation of our hearts. They tally exactly with the present circumstances of mankind, and are admirably adapted to cure every disease, every disorder of the human mind, to beget, to cherish, and confirm every pure, every virtuous, every pious disposition.

Mankind are certainly at present in a state of the deepest corruption and depravity, and at the same time apt to continue strangely insensible of the misery and danger to which, under the government of infinite Wisdom, it necessarily renders them. Nothing can be conceived more fit to rouse them from their lethargy, and to awaken them

them to a just sense of their condition, than a messenger from Heaven, clothed with divine authority, setting before them the intrinsic baseness, malignity, and wretchedness of vice, together with the certain, the dreadful, the eternal consequences of continuing in it.

Could we enter upon a particular view of all those maladies, and disorders which infest and destroy the souls of men, it were easy to shew, that a stedfast belief of religion, is in truth, the most natural and the best antidote or remedy for each of them. It is obvious, at least, that the clear and full manifestation, which the gospel has given of the character of God, and the laws of his moral government, and of the terms of salvation through faith in the religion of his son, are all finely calculated to root out the principles of superstition, and all false notions, destructive to the virtue and happiness of mankind, and to plant in their room whatever has a natural and direct tendency to promote our virtue, our perfection, our felicity.

M.

(2) Cleomenes, king of Sparta, when suffering under misfortune, was advised to kill himself by Tharyceon. "Thinkest thou, wicked man, (said

(said he) to shew thy fortitude by rushing upon death, an expedient always at hand, the dastardly resource of the basest minds? Better than we, by the fortune of arms, or overpowered by numbers, have left the field of battle to their enemies; but he who, to avoid pain or calamity, or from a slavish regard to the praise or censures of men, gives up the contest, is overcome by his own cowardice. If we are to seek death, that death ought to be in action. It is base to live or die only for ourselves. All we gain by suicide is to get rid of present difficulty, without increasing our own reputation, or doing the least service to our country. In hopes, then, we may yet be of some use to others, both methinks are bound to preserve life as long as we can. Whenever these hopes shall have altogether abandoned us, death, if sought for, will readily be found."

(3) Of all the refined cobwebs, to which sophistry has given birth, this seems at once the most elaborate and the most flimsy. It seems one of the first and most indisputable maxims in all sound reasoning, that no ideas whatever should have a place in the premises, which do not communicate a sensible energy to the conclusion. But where is the connection between the beginning and end of this wire drawn argument. What

have

have the various beautiful facts, thus elegantly stated, to do with a man's taking away his own life? Though the greatest philosopher be of no more consequence to the general system of things than an oyster, and though the life of the one were, in every respect, as perfectly insignificant as that of the other, still the meanest of mankind is not without importance in his own eyes. And where is he who is guided uniformly in all his actions, more by a sense of his relation to the universe at large, than by the value he retains for himself, or the deference he has to his own opinion.

No deduction, however plausible, can produce conviction in any rational mind, which originates in a supposition grossly absurd. Is it possible to conceive the author of nature capable of authenticating a deed, which ultimately terminates in the total annihilation of the system? By which of the creatures beneath us is the first law of their being thus daringly violated? And if suicide be eligible to man, under any possible misfortune or distress, why not to them? Are not they also subject to the various miseries which arise from wayward accidents and hostile elements? Why, therefore, open a door for our escape from those evils of which others have

their

their share; to whom, however, it must remain for ever shut?

In truth, the existence of all animals depends entirely on their inviolable attachment to self-preservation. Their attention to all possible means of self-defence and sustenance, is accordingly the obvious and common condition of all their natures. By this great and operative principle nature has chiefly consulted her own safety. Our philosophers notions are so extremely hostile to her most essential institutions, that she could not possibly survive a general conviction of them. And, in spite of all the sophistry he is master of, the question here will eternally recur, whether the wisdom of nature, or the philosophy of our author, deserves the preference.

(4) This apology for the commission, arising from man's insignificance in the moral world, from the reciprocation of social duty being dissolved, or from the benefit resulting from the voluntary dismission of being, is contrary to the soundest principles of jurisprudence, to the condition of human nature, and to the general establishment of things.

That a man who retires from life *ad libitum*, does no harm to society, is a proposition peculiarly absurd and erroneous. What is lawful for

for one, may be lawful for all, and no society can subsist in the conviction of a principle thus hostile to its being.

It seems to be a maxim in human existence, that no creature has a right to decide peremptorily on the importance, utility or necessity of his own being. There are an infinite variety of secret connections and associations in the vast system of things, which the eye of created wisdom cannot explore.

Man is not, perhaps, so ignorant of any thing, or any creature, as of himself. His own system, after all the art and inquisition of human ingenuity, is still to him the profoundest mystery in nature. His knowledge and faculties are adequate to the sphere of his duty. Beyond this, his researches are impertinent, and all his acquisitions useless. He has no adequate notions what the laws of the universe are with respect to any species of existence whatever. A cloud rests on the complicated movements of this great machine, which baffles all the penetration of mortals: and it will for ever remain impossible for man, from the most complete analysis of his present situation, to judge, with any degree of precision, of his own consequence, either

ther as a citizen of the world at large, or as a member of any particular society.

FINAL causes form a system of knowledge too wonderful for man. It is the prerogative of nature alone to decide upon them. In the fulness of time, her creative hand brought him into existence; and it belongs to her alone, in consequence of an arrangement equally wonderful and mysterious, to dismiss him from his present mode of being. This is an authority with which she alone is invested, and which, according to our apprehensions, it is impossible for her to delegate. Dissolution, as well as creation, is hers, and he who would attempt to infringe her sovereignty in this instance, would usurp a prerogative which does not belong to him, and become a traitor to the laws of his being. Nay, on this extravagant and licentious hypothesis, the right of assuming and relinquishing existence is made reciprocal. For he who arrogates the liberty of destroying himself, were he possessed of the power, might also be his own creator; his imaginary insignificance to society being as inconclusive in the one case, as any chimerical advantage that may accidentally strike him can be in the other. It is a strange doctrine, which cannot be established but at the

obvious

obvious expence of what seem the plainest dictates of common sense.

INDEED, the absurdities of this daring and paradoxical doctrine are endless and infinite.—When we come to pronounce on the condition of human infancy, and to separate childhood, or non-age, from a state of maturity, we can scarce trace one useful or salutary consequence it is calculated to produce in society. In this view children seem less adapted to serve any special or important end, than even beetles, gnats, or flies. Experience, however, has long convinced the world of their present inestimable value from their future destination. And were a legislator, from the plausible pretext of their being a burden to the state, to exterminate the race of mankind in the insignificant stage of infancy, his decree, like that of a certain monster recorded in the gospel, would shock the sentiments of every nation under heaven, in whom there remained only the dregs of humanity.

IT is not only impossible for a man to decide, in any given period, of the progress of his existence, or what utility or consequence he may be to society; but without the faculty of prescience, it is still more impracticable for him to divine what purposes he may be intended to

F

serve

serve in the many mysterious revelations of futurity. How far his mortal may be connected with his immortal life, must rest with him who has the sole disposal of it. But who told him that his load of misery was too much to bear, that he was not able to sustain it? or that his merciful Father would not proportionate his sufferings to his abilities? How does he know how short-lived the pressure of incumbent sorrow may prove? It becomes not him to prescribe to his Maker, or because his evils are enormous, to conclude they must be permanent. Rash man! thy heart is in the hand of heaven, and he *who tempers the wind to the shorn lamb*, may either lighten the burthen that oppresses thee, or blunt the edge of that sensibility, from which it derives the greatest poignancy. What medicine is to the wounds of the body, that resignation is to those of the soul. Be not deficient in this virtue, and life will never prescribe a duty you cannot perform, or inflict a pang which you cannot bear. Resignation changes the grizzly aspect of affliction, turns sickness into health, and converts the gloomy forebodings of despair into the grateful presentiments of hope. Besides, the most insignificant instruments are sometimes, in the hands of eternal Providence, employed in bringing about the most general and beneficent revolu-

revolutions. It is by making weakness thus subservient to power, evil to good, and pain to pleasure, that he who governs the world illustrates his sovereignty and omnipotence. Till, then, thou art able to comprehend the whole mysterious system of every possible existence, till thou art certain that thy life is totally insignificant, till thou art convinced it is not in the might of infinite Power to render thee serviceable either to thyself or others, counteract not the benignity of providence by suicide; or, in this manner, by the blackest of all treasons, betray thy trust, and wage at fearful odds, hostility against the very means and author of thy being.

ONE very obvious consequence arising from suicide, which none of its advocates appear to have foreseen, and which places it in a light exceedingly gross and shocking, is, that it supposes every man capable, not only of destroying himself, but of delegating the power of committing murder to another. That which he may do himself, he may commission any one to do for him. On this supposition, no law human or divine, could impeach the shedding of innocent blood. And on what principle of right or expediency, admit that which produces such a train of the most horrid and detestable consequences?

(5) The preceding note is, perhaps, the most audacious part in the whole of this very extraordinary performance. In our holy religion it is expressly declared, that no murderer hath eternal life abiding in him; that murderers shall in no wise inherit the kingdom of God, and that it is the prerogative of heaven alone to kill and make alive. It is a fundamental doctrine in the gospel, that, except ye repent, ye shall all likewise perish. And how are they to perform their duty, who, in the instant of dying, contract a guilt, which renders it indispensible. But this horrid supposition is repugnant to the whole genius of revelation, which inculcates every virtue that can possibly administer to our present and future welfare. It inforces obedience and resignation to the righteous government of God. It inspires and produces those very dispositions which it recommends. All its doctrines, exhortations, and duties, are formed to elevate the mind; to raise the affections, to regulate the passions, and to purge the heart of whatever is hostile to happiness in this or another life. This impious slander on the christian faith is the obvious consequence of the grossest inattention to its nature and tendency. It is calculated chiefly to make us happy. And

what

what happy man was ever yet chargeable with suicide? In short, we may as well say, that, because the physician does not expresly prohibit certain diseases in his prescriptions, the very diseases are authenticated by the remedies devised, on purpose to counteract them.

# IMMORTALITY OF THE SOUL.

(1) THE ingenuity of Scepticism has been long admired, but here the author boldly out-does all his former out-doings. Much has been said against the authenticity of religion, on the supposition that the evidence to which she appeals, is not either sufficiently general or intelligible to the bulk of mankind. But surely an argument is not conclusive in one case, and inconclusive in another. Admit this reasoning against revelation to be valid, and you must also admit it against our author's hypothesis. There never at least was an objection started that could, in the remotest degree, affect the truths of the gospel, more intricate, metaphysical, and abstracted, than that by which our essayist would destroy the popular doctrine of the soul's *immortality*. How many live and die in this salutary conviction, to whom these refined speculations must for ever remain as unintelligible as if they had never been

been formed! It is a sentiment so congenial to the heart of man, that few of the species would chuse to exist without it. Unable, as they are, to account for its origin, they cordially and universally indulge it, as one of their tenderest, best, and last feelings. It inhabits alike the rudest and most polished minds, and never leaves any human breast, which is not either wholly engrossed by criminal pleasure, deadened by selfish pursuits, or perverted by false reasoning. It governs with all the ardour and influence of inspiration, and never meets with any opposition but from the weak, the worthless, or the *wise above what is written*. All the world have uniformly considered it as their last resource in every extremity, and for the most part still regard and cherish the belief of it, as an asylum in which their best interests are ultimately secured or deposited, beyond the reach of all temporary disaster or misfortune. Where therefore, is the probability of exterminating so popular and prevailing a notion, by a concatenation of ideas, which, perhaps, not one out of a million in any country under Heaven is able to trace or comprehend?

(2). The natural perceptions of pleasure or pain cannot be said to act on the mind as one part of matter does on another. The substance of the

the soul we do not know, but are certain her ideas must be immaterial. And these cannot possibly act either by contact or impulse. When one body impels another, the body moved is affected only by the impulse. But the mind, whenever roused by any pleasing or painful sensation, in most cases looks round her, and deliberates whether a change of state is proper, or the present more eligible; and moves or rests accordingly. Her perceptions, therefore, contribute no further to action, than by exciting her active powers. On the contrary, matter is blindly and obstinately in that state in which it is, whether of motion or rest, till changed by some other adequate cause. Suppose we rest the state of any body, some external force is requisite to put it in motion; and, in proportion as this force is greater or small, the motion must be swift or slow. Did not this body continue in its former state, no external force would be requisite to change it; nor, when changed, would different degrees of force be necessary to move it in different degrees of velocity. When motion is impressed on any body, to bring it to rest, an *extra*-force must always be applied, in proportion to the intended effect. This resistance is observable in bodies both when moved in particular directions, and to bear an exact proportion to the *vis impressa*, and to the quantity of matter

ter

ter moved. Were it possible to extract from matter the qualities of solidity and extension, the matter whence such qualities were extracted would no longer resist; and consequently resistance is the necessary result of them, which, therefore, in all directions must be the same. The degree of resistance in any body being proportionate to the *vis impressa*, it follows, when that body is considered in any particular state, whether of motion or rest, the degrees of resistance must either indefinitely multiply or decrease, according to all possible degrees of the moving force. But when the same body is considered absolutely, or without fixing any particular state, the resistance is immutable; and all the degrees of it, which that body would exert upon the accession of any impressed force, must be conceived as actually in it. Nor can matter have any tendency contrary to that resistance, otherwise it must be equal or superior. If equal, the two contrary tendencies would destroy each other. If superior, the resistance would be destroyed. Thus change would eternally succeed to change without one intermediate instant, so that no time would be assigned when any body was in any particular state. Gravitation itself, the most simple and universal law, seems far from being a tendency natural to matter; since it is found to act internally, and not in proportion

to

to the superficies of any body; which it would not do, if it were only the mechanical action of matter upon matter. From all this, it appears, that matter considered merely as such, is so far from having a principle of spontaneous motion, that it is stubbornly inactive, and must eternally remain in the same state in which it happens to be, except influenced by some other—that is, some immaterial power. Of such a power the human soul is evidently possessed; for every one is conscious of an internal activity, and to dispute this would be to dispute us out of one of the most real and intimate perceptions we have.

Though a material automaton were allowed possible, how infinitely would it fall short of that force and celerity which every one feels in himself. How sluggish are all the movements which fall under our observation. How slow and gradual their transitions from one part of space to another. But the mind, by one instantaneous effort, measures the distance from pole to pole, from heaven to earth, from one fixed star to another; and not confined within the limits of the visible creation, shoots into immensity with a rapidity to which even that of lightning, or sun-beams, is no comparison. Who then shall assign a period, which, though depressed with so much dead weight, is ever active, and unconscious

of

of fatigue or relaxation? The mind is not only herself a principle of action, but probably actuates the body, without the affistance of any intermediate power, both from the gradual command which she acquires of its members by habit, and from a capacity of determining, in some meafure, the quantity of pleafure or pain which any fenfible perception can give her. Suppofing the interpofing power a fpirit, the fame difficulty of fpirit acting upon matter ftill remains. And the volition of our own mind will as well account for the motion of the body, as the formal interference of any other fpiritual fubftance. And we may as well afk, why the mind is not confcious of that interpofition, as why fhe is ignorant of the means by which fhe communicates motion to the body.

(3) It is always bad reafoning to draw conclufions from the premifes not denied by your adverfary. Whoever, yet, of all the affertors of the foul's immortality, prefumed to make a monopoly of this great privilege to the human race? Who can tell what another ftate of exiftence may be, or whether every other fpecies of animals may not poffefs principles as immortal as the mind of man? But that mode of reafoning, which militates againft all our convictions, folely on account of the unavoidable ignorance

to which our sphere in the universe subjects us, can never be satisfactory. Reason, it is true, cannot altogether solve every doubt which arises concerning this important truth. But neither is there any other truth, of any denomination whatever, against which sophistry may not conjure up a multitude of exceptions. We know no mode of existence but those of matter and spirit, neither of which has uniformly and successfully defied the extreme subtilty of argumentation. Still a very great majority of mankind are staunch believers in both. So well constituted is the present disposition of things, that all the principles essential to human life and happiness continue, as it is likely they ever will, to operate, in spite of every sort of clamour which sophistry or scepticism has raised or can raise against them.

(4) There is not a single word in all this elaborate and tedious deduction, which has not been urged and refuted five hundred times. Our ignorance of the divine perfections, as is usual with this writer, is here stated as an unanswerable exception to the conclusion usually drawn from them. But he very artfully overlooks, that this great ignorance will be equally conclusive as applied to either side of the argument. When we compare, however, the character of God, as

a wise

a wise superintendant, and generous benefactor, with the state in which things at present appear, where virtue is often depressed and afflicted, and vice apparently triumphs, it will be treated with the infamy it merits, and virtue receive that happiness and honour, which, from its own intrinsic worth, it deserves, and, from its conformity to the nature of God, it has reason to expect.

This subject, perhaps, has been too much exaggerated, and some pious men have weakly thought, the best way to convince us that order and happiness prevailed in a future state, was to persuade us that there was none at all in this. External advantages have been taken for the only goods of human nature; and, because, in this view, all things speak the appearance of mal-administration, we have been taught to expect a government of rectitude and benevolence hereafter. Let us, on the contrary, candidly own that virtue is sovereignly and solely good, lest, by depreciating her charms, we obliquely detract from the character of God himself. Let us confess her undowered excellence superior to all the inconveniences that may attend her, even in the present situation. But, without allowing some difference between poverty and riches, sickness and health, pain and pleasure, &c. we shall have no founda-

G tion

tion to preference; and it will be in vain to talk of selecting where no one choice can be more agreeable or disagreeable to nature than another. Upon this difference, therefore, however it be called, let the present argument proceed.

If infinite Goodness be the spirit and characteristic of this universal government, then every advantage, however inconsiderable in kind or degree, must either be supposed immediately bestowed on virtue; or, at least, that such retributions will, at some time, be made her, as may not only render her votaries equal, but superior to those of vice, in proportion to their merit. But how different the case is in human life, history and observation may easily convince us; so that one, whose eyes are not intent on the character of God, and the nature of virtue, would often be tempted to think this world a theatre merely intended for mournful spectacles and pomps of horror. How many persons do we see perish by the mere wants of nature, who, had they been in different circumstances, would have thanked God with tears of joy for the power of communicating those advantages they now implore from others in vain? While, at the same time, they have, perhaps, the additional misery of seeing the most endeared relations involved in the same deplorable fate! How

often

often do we see those ties which unite the soul and body, worn out by the gradual advances of a lingering disease, or burst at once by the sudden efforts of unutterable agony? While the unhappy sufferers, had they been continued in life, might have diffused happiness, not only through the narrow circle of their friends and neighbourhood, but as extensively as their country, and even the world at large. How many names do we see buried in obscurity, or soiled with detraction, which ought to have shone the first in fame? How many heroes have survived the liberties of their country, or died in abortive attempts to preserve them; and by their fall, only left a larger field for the lawless ravages of tyranny and oppression?

But were it possible, how long and insuperable would be the task to enumerate all the ingredients which compose the present cup of bitterness? And is this the consummation of things? Will supreme and essential Goodness no way distinguish such as have invariably pursued his honour, and the interest of his government, from those who have industriously violated the order he has appointed in things? who have blotted the face of nature with havock, murder, and desolation; and shewn a constant intention to counteract all the benevolent designs of Providence? It is confessed

that

that the virtuous, happy in the possession of virtue alone, make their exit from the present scene with blessings to their Creator, for having called them to existence, and given them the glorious opportunity of enjoying what is in itself supremely eligible. They are conscious that this felicity can receive no accession from any external lustre or advantage whatever. Yet it seems highly necessary in the divine administration, that those who have been dazzled with the false glare of prosperous wickedness, should at last be undeceived; that they should at last behold virtue conspicuous, in all her native splendor and majesty as she shines, the chief delight of God, and ultimate happiness of all-intelligent nature.

The language of religion, and our own hearts, on this important argument, is equally comfortable and decisive. It accumulates and enforces whatever can inspire us with confidence in that God, who is not the God of the dead, but of the living; who reigns in the invisible, as well as in the visible world; and whose attention to our welfare ceases not with our lives, but is commensurate to the full extent of our being. Indeed the votaries of the soul's mortality may as well be honest for once, and speak out what so many fools think in their hearts. For what is God to us, us, or we to him, if our connection extends but to the pitiful space allotted us in such a pitiful world as this is? To be sure, no abſurdity will be rejected, which can ſmother the feelings, or keep the vices of profligates in countenance; but, if only made like worms and reptiles beneath our feet, to live this moment, and expire the next, to ſtruggle in a wretched life with every internal and external calamity, that can aſſault our bodies or infeſt our minds; to bear the mortifications of malignity, and the unmerited abhorrence of thoſe who perhaps may owe us the greateſt and tendereſt eſteem, and then, ſunk in everlaſting oblivion, our fate would ſtand on record, in the annals of the univerſe, an eternal exception to all that can be called good.

Suppoſe a father poſſeſſed of the moſt exquiſite tenderneſs for his ſon, delighted with his ſimilarity of form, his promiſing conſtitution, his ſtrength, gracefulneſs, and agility, his undiſguiſed emotions of filial affection, with the various preſages of a ſuperior genius and underſtanding. Let us ſuppoſe this father pleaſed with the employment of improving his faculties, and inſpiring him with future hopes of happineſs and dignity: but that he may give him a quicker ſenſibility to the misfortunes of others, and a more unſhaken fortitude

fortitude to sustain his own, he often prefers younger brethren, and even strangers, to those advantages which otherwise merit, and the force of nature would determine him to bestow on so worthy an offspring. Let us go further, and imagine, if we can, that this father, without the least diminution of tenderness, or any other apparent reason, destroys his son in the bloom of life, and height of expectation: Who would not lament the fate of such a youth with inconsolable tears? Doomed never more to behold the agreeable light of Heaven! never more to display his personal graces, nor exercise his manly powers; never more to feel his heart warm with benevolent regards, nor taste the soul-transporting pleasure of obliging and being obliged! Blotted at once from existence, and the fair creation, he sinks into silence and oblivion, with all his sublime hopes disappointed, all his immense desires ungratified, and all his intellectual faculties unimproved. Without mentioning the instinctive horror which must attend such an action, how absurd to reason, and how inconsistent with the common feelings of humanity, would it be to suppose a father capable of such a deed. Forbid it God! forbid it, Nature! that we should impute to the munificent Father of being and happiness, what, even in the lowest of rational creatures, would be monstrous and detestable!

(5) The

(5) The truth is, that form which all mankind have deemed immortal, is so far from being the frailest, that it seems in fact the most indissoluble and permanent of any other we know. All the rational and inventive powers of the mind happily conspire to proclaim her infinitely different in nature, and superior in dignity to every possible modification of pure matter. Were mankind joined in society, was life polished and cultivated, were the sciences and arts, not only of utility, but elegance, produced by matter? by brute mass? A substance so contrary to all activity, and intelligence, that it seems the work of an omnipotent hand alone to connect them. What judgment should we form of that principle which informed and enlightened a Galileo, a Copernicus, or a Newton? What inspiration taught them, to place the sun in the centre of this system, and assign the various orbs their revolutions round him, reducing motions so diverse and unequal to uniform and simple laws? Was it not something like that great eternal mind, which first gave existence to those luminous orbs, and prescribed each of them their province? Whence the infinite harmony and variety of sound, the copious flows of eloquence, the bolder graces and more inspired elevations of poetry, but from a mind, an immaterial being, the reflected image of her all-perfect Creator, in whom eternally dwells all beauty and excellence. Were

man

man only endowed with a principle of vegetation, fixed to one peculiar spot, and infensible of all that paffed around him; we might, then, with fome colour, fuppofe that energy, if it may be fo called, perifhable. Were he, like animals, poffeffed of mere vitality, and qualified only to move and feel, ftill we might have fome reafon to fear that, in fome future period of duration, our Creator might refume his gift of exiftence. But can any one, who pretends to the leaft reflection, imagine that fuch a being as the human foul, adorned with fuch extenfive intellectual powers, will ever ceafe to be the object of that love and care which eternally holds the univerfe in its embrace? Did fhe obtain fuch a boundlefs underftanding merely to tafte the pleafure of exercifing it? to catch a tranfient glance of its objects, and perifh? Formed, as fhe is, to operate on herfelf, and all things round her, muft fhe ceafe from action, while yet the mighty tafk is fcarce begun? muft fhe lofe thofe faculties, by which fhe retains the paft, comprehends the prefent, and prefages the future? muft fhe contemplate no more thofe bright impreffions of divinity, which are difcovered in the material world; nor thofe ftronger, and more animated features of the fame eternal beauty which fhine in her own god-like form? And muft fhe be abforbed for ever in the womb of uneffential nothing? Strange, that in the view, and even in the arms

of

of infinite power and goodness, a dawn so fair and promising, should at once be clouded with all the horrors of eternal night? Such a supposition would be contrary to the whole conduct and laws of nature.

*The following Letters on* SUICIDE *are extracted from* ROSSEAU's ELOISA.

## LETTER CXIV.

*To Lord B——.*

YES, my lord, I confess it; the weight of life is too heavy for my soul. I have long endured it as a burden; I have lost every thing which could make it dear to me, and nothing remains but irksomeness and vexation. I am told, however, that I am not at liberty to dispose of my life, without the permission of that Being from whom I received it. I am sensible likewise that you have a right over it by more titles than one. Your care has twice preserved it, and your goodness is its constant security. I will never dispose of it, till I am certain that I may do it without a crime, and till I have not the least hope of employing it for your service.

You

You told me that I should be of use to you; why did you deceive me? Since we have been in London, so far from thinking of employing me in your concerns, you have been kind enough to make me your only concern. How superfluous is your obliging solicitude? My lord, you know I abhor a crime, even worse than I detest life; I adore the supreme Being—I owe every thing to you; I have an affection for you; you are the only person on earth to whom I am attached. Friendship and duty may chain a wretch to this earth: sophistry and vain pretences will never detain him. Enlighten my understanding, speak to my heart; I am ready to hear you, but remember, that despair is not to be imposed upon.

You would have me apply to the test of reason; I will, let us reason. You desire me to deliberate in proportion to the importance of the question in debate; I agree to it. Let us investigate truth
with

with temper and moderation; let us discuss this general proposition with the same indifference we should treat any other. Robeck wrote an apology for suicide before he put an end to his life. I will not, after his example, write a book on the subject, neither am I well satisfied with that which he has penned, but I hope in this discussion at least to imitate his moderation.

I have for a long time meditated on this awful subject. You must be sensible that I have, for you know my destiny, and yet I am alive. The more I reflect, the more I am convinced that the question may be reduced to this fundamental proposition: Every man has a right by nature to pursue what he thinks good, and avoid what he thinks evil, in all respects which are not injurious to others. When our life therefore becomes a misery to ourselves, and is of advantage to no one, we are at liberty to put an end to our being. If there is any such thing as a clear and self-
evident

evident principle, certainly this is one; and if this be subverted, there is scarce an action in life which may not be made criminal.

Let us hear what the philosophers say on this subject. First, they consider life as something which is not our own, because we hold it as a gift; but because it has been given to us, is it for that reason our own? Has not God given these sophists two arms? nevertheless, when they are under apprehensions of a mortification, they do not scruple to amputate one, or both, if there be occasion. By a parity of reasoning, we may convince those who believe in the immortality of the soul; for if I sacrifice my arm to the preservation of something more precious, which is my body, I have the same right to sacrifice my body to the preservation of something more valuable, which is, the happiness of my existence. If all the gifts which heaven has bestowed are naturally designed for our good, they are certainly too apt to change their nature; and Providence has endowed us with reason, that we may discern the difference. If this rule did not authorise us to chuse the one, and reject the other, to what use would it serve among mankind?

But they turn this weak objection into a thousand shapes. They consider a man living upon earth as a soldier placed on duty. God, say they, has fixed you in this world, why do you quit your station without his leave? But you, who argue thus, has he not stationed you in the town where you was born, why therefore do you quit it without his leave? Is not misery, of itself, a sufficient permission? Whatever station Providence has assigned me, whether it be in a regiment, or on the earth at large, he intended me to stay there while I found my situation agreeable, and to leave it when it became intollerable. This is the voice of nature, and the voice of God. I agree, that we must wait for an

order;

order; but when I die a natural death, God does not order me to quit life, he takes it from me; it is by rendering life infupportable, that he orders me to quit it. In the firft cafe, I refift with all my force; in the fecond, I have the merit of obedience.

Can you conceive that there are fome people fo abfurd as to arraign fuicide as a kind of rebellion againft Providence, by an attempt to fly from his laws? But we do not put an end to our being in order to withdraw ourfelves from his commands, but to execute them. What! does the power of God extend no farther than to my body? Is there a fpot in the univerfe, is there any being in the univerfe, which is not fubject to his power, and will that power have lefs immediate influence over me when my being is refined, and thereby becomes lefs compound, and of nearer refemblance to the divine effence? No, his juftice and goodnefs are the foundation of my hopes;

and,

and, if I thought that death would withdraw me from his power, I would give up my resolution to die.

This is one of the quibbles of the Phædo, which, in other respects, abounds with sublime truths. If your slave destroys himself, says Socrates to Cebes, would you not punish him, for having unjustly deprived you of your property; prithee, good Socrates, do we not belong to God after we are dead? The case you put is not applicable; you ought to argue thus: If you incumber your slave with a habit which confines him from discharging his duty properly, will you punish him for quitting it, in order to render you better service? The grand error lies in making life of too great importance; as if our existence depended upon it, and that death was a total annihilation. Our life is of no consequence in the sight of God; it is of no importance in the eyes of reason, neither ought it to be of any in our sight; when we

quit

quit our body, we only lay aside an inconvenient habit. Is this circumstance so painful, to be the occasion of so much disturbance? My Lord, these decleimers are not in earnest; their arguments are absurd and cruel, for they aggravate the supposed crime, as if it put a period to existence, and they punish it, as if that existence was eternal.

With respect to Plato's Phædo, which has furnished them with the only specious argument that has ever been advanced, the question is discussed there in a very light and desultory manner. Socrates being condemned, by an unjust judgment, to lose his life in a few hours, had no occasion to enter into an accurate enquiry whether he was at liberty to dispose of it himself. Supposing him really to have been the author of those discourses which Plato ascribes to him, yet believe me, my Lord, he would have meditated with more attention on the subject, had he been in circumstances which

which required to reduce his speculations to practice; and a strong proof that no valid objection can be drawn from that immortal work against the right of disposing of our own lives, is, that Cato read it twice through the very night that he destroyed himself.

The same sophisters make it a question, whether life can ever be an evil? But when we consider the multitude of errors, torments, and vices, with which it abounds, one would rather be inclined to doubt whether it can ever be a blessing. Guilt incessantly besieges the most virtuous of mankind. Every moment he lives he is in danger of falling a prey to the wicked, or of being wicked himself. To struggle and to endure, is his lot in this world; that of the dishonest man is to do evil, and to suffer. In every other particular they differ, and only agree in sharing the miseries of life in common. If you required authorities and facts, I could recite you the oracles of old, the answers of the sages,

and

and produce instances where acts of virtue have been recompensed with death. But let us leave these considerations, my lord; it is to you whom I address myself, and I ask you what is the chief attention of a wise man in this life, except, if I may be allowed the expression, to collect himself inwardly, and endeavour even while he lives, to be dead to every object of sense? The only way by which wisdom directs us to avoid the miseries of human nature, is it not to detach ourselves from all earthly objects, from every thing that is gross in our composition, to retire within ourselves, and to raise our thoughts to sublime contemplations? If therefore our misfortunes are derived from our passions and errors, with what eagerness should we wish for a state which will deliver us both from the one and the other? What is the fate of those sons of sensuality, who indiscreetly multiply their torments by their pleasures; they in fact destroy their existence by extending their connections in this life;

they

they increase the weight of their crimes by their numerous attachments; they relish no enjoyments, but what are succeeded by a thousand bitter wants; the more lively their sensibility, the more acute their sufferings; the stronger they are attached to life, the more wretched they become.

But admitting it, in general, a benefit to mankind to crawl upon the earth with gloomy sadness, (I do not mean to intimate that the human race ought with one common consent to destroy themselves, and make the world one immense grave) there are miserable beings who are too much exalted to be governed by vulgar opinion; to them despair and grievous torments are the passports of nature. It would be as ridiculous to suppose that life can be a blessing to such men, as it was absurd in the sophister Possidonius to deny that it was an evil, at the same time that he endured all the torments of the gout. While life is agreeable to us

we

we earnestly wish to prolong it, and nothing but a sense of extreme misery can extinguish the desire of existence; for we naturally conceive a violent dread of death, and this dread conceals the miseries of human nature from our sight. We drag a painful and melancholy life, for a long time, before we can resolve to quit it; but when once life becomes so insupportable as to overcome the horror of death, then existence is evidently a great evil, and we cannot disengage ourselves from it too soon. Therefore, though we cannot exactly ascertain the point at which it ceases to be a blessing, yet at least we are certain that it is an evil long before it appears to be such, and with every sensible man the right of quitting life is, by a great deal, precedent to the temptation.

This is not all. After they have denied that life can be an evil, in order to bar our right of making away with ourselves; they confess immediately afterwards,

terwards, that it is an evil, by reproaching us with want of courage to support it. According to them, it is cowardice to withdraw ourselves from pain and trouble, and there are none but dastards who destroy themselves. O Rome, thou victrix of the world, what a race of cowards did thy empire produce! let Arria, Eponina, Lucretia, be of the number; they were women. But Brutus, Cassius, and thou great and divine Cato, who didst share with the gods the adoration of an astonished world, thou whose sacred and august presence animated the Romans with holy zeal, and made tyrants tremble, little did thy proud admirers imagine that paltry rhetoricians, immured in the dusty corner of a college, would ever attempt to prove that thou wert a coward, for having preferred death to a shameful existence.

O the dignity and energy of your modern writers! how sublime, how intrepid are you with your pens? But tell me, thou

thou great and valiant hero, who dost so courageously decline the battle, in order to endure the pain of living somewhat longer; when a spark of fire lights upon your hand, why do ye withdraw it in such haste? how? are you such a coward that you dare not bear the scorching of fire? Nothing, you say, can oblige you to endure the burning spark; and what obliges me to endure life? Was the creation of a man of more difficulty to Providence than that of a straw? and is not both one and the other equally the work of his hands?

Without doubt, it is an evidence of great fortitude to bear with firmness the misery which we cannot shun; none but a fool, however, will voluntarily endure evils which he can avoid without a crime; and it is very often a great crime to suffer pain unnecessarily. He who has not resolution to deliver himself from a miserable being by a speedy death, is like one who would rather suffer a wound to mortify, than trust to a surgeon's knife for his cure. Come, thou worthy ———, cut off this leg, which endan-

endangers my life; I will see it done without shrinking, and will give that hero leave to call me coward, who suffers his leg to mortify, because he dares not undergo the same operation.

I acknowledge that there are duties owing to others, the nature of which will not allow every man to dispose of his life: but, in return, how many are there which give him a right to dispose of it. Let a magistrate on whom the welfare of a nation depends, let a father of a family who is bound to procure subsistence for his children, let a debtor who might ruin his creditors, let these at all events discharge their duty. Admitting a thousand other civil and domestic relations to oblige an honest and unfortunate man to support the misery of life, to avoid the greater evil of doing injustice; is it, therefore, under circumstances totally different, incumbent on us to preserve a life oppressed with a swarm of miseries, when it can be of no service but to him who has not courage to die? " Kill me, " my child," says the decrepid savage to his

his son, who carries him on his shoulders, and bends under his weight, " the enemy " is at hand; go to battle with thy bre- " thren; go and preserve thy children, and " do not suffer thy helpless father to fall " alive into the hands of those whose re- " lations he has mangled." Though hunger, sickness, and poverty, those domestic plagues, more dreadful than savage enemies, may allow a wretched cripple to consume, in a sick bed, the provisions of a family which can scarce subsist itself, yet he who has no connections, whom Heaven has reduced to the necessity of living alone, whose wretched existence can produce no good, why should not he, at least, have the right of quitting a station, where his complaints are troublesome, and his sufferings of no benefit?

Weigh these considerations, my lord; collect these arguments, and you will find that they may be reduced to the most simple of nature's rights, of which no man of sense ever yet entertained a doubt. In fact, why should we be allowed to cure ourselves of the gout, and not to get rid of

the

the misery of life? Do not both evils proceed from the same hand? To what purpose is it to say, that death is painful? Are drugs agreeable to be taken? No, nature revolts against both. Let them prove therefore that it is more justifiable to cure a transient disorder by the application of remedies, than to free ourselves from an incurable evil by putting an end to our life; and let them shew how it can be less criminal to use the bark for a fever, than to take opium for the stone. If we consider the object in view, it is in both cases to free ourselves from painful sensations; if we regard the means, both one and the other are equally natural; if we consider the repugnance of our nature, it operates equally on both sides; if we attend to the will of Providence, can we struggle against any evil of which it is not the author? can we deliver ourselves from any torment which the hand of God has not inflicted? What are the bounds which limit his power, and when is resistance lawful? Are we then to make no alteration in the condition of things, because every thing

thing is in the state he appointed? Must we do nothing in this life, for fear of infringing his laws, or is it in our power to break them if we would? No, my lord, the occupation of man is more great and noble. God did not give him life that he should supinely remain in a state of constant inactivity. But he gave him freedom to act, conscience to will, and reason to choose what is good. He has constituted him sole judge of all his actions. He has engraved this precept in his heart, do whatever you conceive to be for your own good, provided you thereby do no injury to others. If my sensations tell me that death is eligible, I resist his orders by an obstinate resolution to live; for, by making death desirable, he directs me to put an end to my being.

My lord, I appeal to your wisdom and candour; what more infallible maxims can reason deduce from religion, with respect to suicide? If Christians have adopted contrary tenets, they are neither drawn from the principles of religion, nor from the

the only sure guide, the Scriptures, but borrowed from the Pagan philosophers. Lactantius and Augustine, the first who propagated this new doctrine, of which Jesus Christ and his apostles take no notice, ground their arguments entirely on the reasoning of Phædo, which I have already controverted; so that the believers, who, in this respect, think they are supported by the authority of the Gospel, are in fact only countenanced by the authority of Plato. In truth, where do we find, throughout the whole Bible, any law against suicide, or so much as a bare disapprobation of it; and is it not very unaccountable, that among the instances produced of persons who devoted themselves to death, we do not find the least word of improbation against examples of this kind? nay, what is more, the instance of Samson's voluntary death is authorised by a miracle, by which he revenges himself of his enemies. Would this miracle have been displayed to justify a crime? And would this man, who lost his strength by suffering himself to be seduced by the al-
lurements

lurements of a woman, have recovered it to commit an authorised crime, as if God himself would practice deceit on men?

Thou shalt do no murder, says the decalogue; what are we to infer from this? If this commandment is to be taken literally, we must not destroy malefactors, nor our enemies: and Moses, who put so many people to death, was a bad interpreter of his own precept. If there are any exceptions, certainly the first must be in favour of suicide, because it is exempt from any degree of violence and injustice, the two only circumstances which can make homicide criminal; and because nature, moreover, has, in this respect, thrown sufficient obstacles in the way.

But still they tell us, we must patiently endure the evils which God inflicts, and make a merit of our sufferings. This application however of the maxims of Christianity, is very ill calculated to satisfy our judgment. Man is subject to a thousand troubles, his life is a complication of evils, and he seems to have been born only to suffer. Reason directs him to shun as many of these evils as he can avoid; and religion, which is never in contradiction to reason, approves of his endeavours. But how inconsiderable is the account of these evils, in comparison with those he is obliged to endure against his will? It is with respect to these, that a merciful God allows man to claim the merit of resistance; he receives the tribute he has been pleased to impose, as a voluntary homage, and he places our resignation in this life to our profit in the next. True repentance is derived from nature; if man endures whatever he is obliged to suffer, he does, in this respect, all that God requires of him; and if any one is so inflated with pride, as to attempt more, he is a madman, who ought to be confined, or an impostor, who ought to be punished. Let us, therefore, without scruple, fly from the evils we can avoid; there will still be too many left for us to endure. Let us, without remorse, quit life itself when it becomes a torment to us, since it is in our own power to do it,

and

and that in so doing we neither offend God nor man. If we would offer a sacrifice to the supreme Being, is it nothing to undergo death? Let us devote to God that which he demands by the voice of reason, and into his hands let us peaceably surrender our souls.

Such are the liberal precepts which good sense dictates to every man, and which religion authorises *. Let us apply these precepts

---

* A strange letter this for the discussion of such a subject! Do men argue so cooly on a question of this nature, when they examine it on their own accounts? Is the letter a forgery, or does the author reason only with an intent to be refuted? What makes our opinion in this particular dubious, is the example of Robeck, which he cites, and which seems to warrant his own. Robeck deliberated so gravely that he had patience to write a book, a large, voluminous, weighty, and dispassionate book; and when he had concluded, according to his principles, that it was lawful to put an end to our being, he destroyed himself with the same composure that he wrote. Let us beware of the prejudices of the times, and of particular countries. When suicide is out of fashion we conclude that none but madmen destroy themselves; and all

precepts to ourselves. You have condescended to disclose your mind to me; I am acquainted with your uneasiness; you do not endure less than myself; and your troubles, like mine, are incurable; and they are the more remediless, as the laws of honour are more immutable than those of fortune. You bear them, I must confess, with fortitude. Virtue supports you; advance but one step farther, and she disengages you. You intreat me to suffer; my lord, I dare importune you to put an end to your sufferings; and I leave you to judge which of us is most dear to the other.

Why should we delay doing that which we must do at last? shall we wait till old age and decrepid baseness attach us to life after all the efforts of courage appear chimerical to dastardly minds; every one judges of others by himself. Nevertheless, how many instances are there, well attested, of men, in every other respect perfectly discreet, who, without remorse, rage, or despair, have quitted life for no other reason than because it was a burden to them, and have died with more composure than they lived?

after they have robbed it of its charms, and till we are doomed to drag an infirm and decrepid body with labour, and ignominy, and pain? We are at an age when the soul has vigour to difengage itfelf with eafe from its fhackles, and when a man knows how to die as he ought; when farther advanced in years, he fuffers himfelf to be torn from life, which he quits with reluctance. Let us take advantage of this time, when the tedium of life makes death defirable; and let us tremble for fear it fhould come in all its horrors, at the moment when we could wifh to avoid it. I remember the time, when I prayed to heaven only for a fingle hour of life, and when I fhould have died in defpair if it had not been granted. Ah! what a pain it is to burft afunder the ties which attach our hearts to this world, and how advifable it is to quit life the moment the connection is broken! I am fenfible, my lord, that we are both worthy of a purer manfion; virtue points it out, and deftiny invites us to feek it. May the friendfhip which invites us preferve

our

our union to the latest hour! O what a pleasure for two sincere friends voluntary to end their days in each others arms, to intermingle their latest breath, and at the same instant to give up the soul which they shared in common! What pain, what regret can infect their last moments? What do they quit by taking leave of the world? They go together; they quit nothing.

## LETTER CXV.

### ANSWER.

THOU art distracted, my friend by a fatal passion; be more discreet; do not give counsel, whilst thou standeth so much in need of advice. I have known greater evils than yours. I am armed with fortitude of mind; I am an Englishman, and not afraid to die; but I know how to live and suffer as becomes a man. I have seen death near at hand, and have viewed it with too much indifference to go in search of it.

It is true, I thought you might be of use to me; my affection stood in need of yours: your endeavours might have been serviceable to me; your understanding might have enlightened me in the most important concern of my life; if I do not

not avail myself of it, who are you to impute it to? Where is it? What is become of it? What are you capable of? Of what use can you be in you present condition? What service can I expect from you? A senseless grief renders you stupid and unconcerned. Thou art no man; thou art nothing; and if I did not consider what thou mightest be, I cannot conceive any thing more abject.

There is need of no other proof than your letter itself. Formerly I could discover in you good sense and truth. Your sentiments were just, your reflections proper, and I liked you not only from judgment but choice; for I considered your influence as an additional motive to excite me to the study of wisdom. But what do I perceive now in the arguments of your letter, with which you appear to be so highly satisfied? A wretched and perpetual sophistry, which in the erroneous deviations of your reason, shews the disorder of your mind, and which I would not stoop to refute, if I did not commiserate your delirium.

To

To subvert all your reasoning with one word, I would only ask you a single question. You who believe in the existence of a God, in the immortality of the soul, and in the free will of man, you surely cannot suppose that an intelligent being is embodied, and stationed on the earth by accident only, to exist, to suffer, and to die. It is certainly most probable that the life of man is not without some design, some end, some moral object. I entreat you to give me a direct answer to this point; after which we will deliberately examine your letter, and you will blush to have written it.

But let us wave all general maxims, about which we often hold violent disputes, without adopting any of them in practice; for in their applications we always find some particular circumstances which make such an alteration in the state of things, that every one thinks himself dispensed from submitting to the rules which he prescribes to others; and it is well known, that every man who establishes general principles, deems them obligatory on all the world, himself excepted. Once more let us speak to you in particular.

You believe that you have a right to put an end to your being. Your proof is of a very singular nature; "because I am disposed to die, say you, I have a right to destroy myself." This is certainly a very convenient argument for villains of all kinds. They ought to be very thankful to you for the arms with which you have furnished them; there can be no crimes, which, according to your arguments, may not be justified by the temptation to perpetrate them; and as soon as the impetuosity of passion shall prevail over the horror of guilt, their disposition to do evil will be considered as a right to commit it.

Is it lawful for you therefore to quit life? I should be glad to know whether you have yet begun to live. What! was you placed here on earth to do nothing

in

in this world? Did not Heaven when it gave you existence give you some task or employment? If you have accomplished your day's work before evening, rest yourself for the remainder of the day; you have a right to do it; but let us see your work. What answer are you prepared to make the supreme Judge, when he demands an account of your time? Tell me, what can you say to him?—I have seduced a virtuous girl: I have forsaken a friend in distress. Thou unhappy wretch! point out to me that just man who can boast that he has lived long enough; let me learn from him in what manner I ought to have spent my days to be at liberty to quit life.

You enumerate the evils of human nature. You are not ashamed to exhaust common-place topics, which have been hackneyed over a hundred times; and you conclude that life is an evil. But search, examine into the order of things, and see whether you can find any good which is not intermingled with evil. Does it therefore follow that there is no good in the universe, and can you confound what is in its own nature evil, with that which is only an evil accidentally? You have confessed yourself, that the transitory and passive life of man is of no consequence, and only bears respect to matter from which he will soon be disencumbered; but his active and moral life, which ought to have most influence over his nature, consist in the exercise of free-will. Life is an evil to a wicked man in prosperity, and a blessing to an honest man in distress; for it is not its casual modification, but its relation to some final object which makes it either good or bad. After all, what are these cruel torments which force you to abandon life? Do you imagine, that under your affected impartiality in the enumeration of the evils of this life, I did not discover that you was ashamed to speak of your own? Trust me, and do not at once abandon every virtue. Preserve at least your wonted sincerity, and speak thus openly to your friend: " I have lost all hope of seducing a mo-

" dest

"dest woman, I am obliged therefore to
"be a man of virtue; I had much ra-
"ther die."

You are weary of living; and you tell me, that life is an evil. Sooner or later you will receive consolation, and then you will say life is a blessing. You will speak with more truth, though not with better reason; for nothing will have altered but yourself. Begin the alteration then from this day; and, since all the evil you lament is in the disposition of your mind, correct your irregular appetites, and do not set your house on fire to avoid the trouble of putting it in order.

I endure misery, say you: Is it in my power to avoid suffering? But this is changing the state of the question: for the subject of enquiry is, not whether you suffer, but whether your life is an evil? Let us proceed. You are wretched, you naturally endeavour to extricate yourself from misery. Let us see whether, for that purpose, it is necessary to die.

Let

Let us for a moment examine the natural tendency of the afflictions of the mind, as in direct opposition to the evils of the body, the two substances being of contrary nature. The latter become worse and more inveterate the longer they continue, and at length utterly destroy this mortal machine. The former, on the contrary, being only external and transitory modifications of an immortal and uncompounded essence, are insensibly effaced, and leave the mind in its original form, which is not susceptible of alteration. Grief, disquietude, regret, and despair, are evils of short duration, which never take root in the mind; and experience always falsifies that bitter reflection, which makes us imagine our misery will have no end. I will go farther; I cannot imagine that the vices which contaminate us, are more inherent in our nature than the troubles we endure; I not only believe that they perish with the body which gives them birth, but I think beyond all doubt, that a longer life would be sufficient to reform mankind, and that many ages of youth would

would teach us that nothing is preferable to virtue.

However this may be, as the greatest part of our physical evils are incessantly encreasing, the acute pains of the body, when they are incurable, may justify a man's destroying himself; for all his faculties being distracted with pain, and the evil being without remedy, he has no longer any use either of his will or of his reason; he ceases to be a man before he is dead, and does nothing more in taking away his life, than quit a body which incumbers him, and in which his soul is no longer resident.

But it is otherwise with the afflictions of the mind, which, let them be ever so acute, always carry their remedy with them. In fact, what is it that makes any evil intolerable? Nothing but its duration. The operations of surgery are generally much more painful than the disorders they cure; but the pain occasioned by the latter is lasting, that of the operation is momentary,

tary, and therefore preferable. What occasion is there therefore for any operation to remove troubles which die of course by their duration, the only circumstance which could render them insupportable? Is it reasonable to apply such desperate remedies to evils which expire of themselves? To a man who values himself on his fortitude, and who estimates years at their real value, of two ways by which he may extricate himself from the same troubles, which will appear preferable, death or time? Have patience, and you will be cured. What would you desire more?

Oh! you will say, it doubles my afflictions to reflect that they will cease at last! This is the vain sophistry of grief! an apophthegm void of reason, of propriety, and perhaps of sincerity. What an absurd motive of despair is the hope of terminating misery*! Even allowing this fantastical

* No, my lord, we do not put an end to misery by these means, but rather fill the measure of affliction, by bursting asunder the last ties which attach us to felicity.

tastical reflection, who would not chuse to encrease the present pain for a moment, under the assurance of putting an end to it, as we scarify a wound in order to heal it? And admitting any charm in grief, to make us in love with suffering, when we release ourselves from it by putting an end to our being, do we not at that instant incur all that we apprehend hereafter?

Reflect thoroughly, young man; what are ten, twenty, thirty years in competition with immortality? Pain and pleasure pass like a shadow; life slides away in an instant; it is nothing of itself; its value depends on the use we make of it. The good that we have done is all that remains, and it is that alone which marks its importance.

Therefore do not say any more that your existence is an evil, since it depends upon felicity. When we regret what was dear to us, grief itself still attaches us to the object we lament, which is a state less deplorable than to be attached to nothing.

upon yourself to make it a blessing; and if it be an evil to have lived, this is an additional reason for prolonging life. Do not pretend neither to say any more that you are at liberty to die; for it is as much as to say that you have power to alter your nature, that you have a right to revolt against the Author of your being, and to frustrate the end of your existence. But when you add, that your death does injury to no one, do you recollect that you make this declaration to your friend?

Your death does injury to no one? I understand you! You think the loss I shall sustain by your death of no importance; you deem my affliction of no consequence. I will urge to you no more the rights of friendship, which you despise; but are there not obligations still more dear*, which ought to induce you to preserve your life? If there be a person in the world who loved you to that degree as to be

---

* Obligations more dear than those of friendship! Is it a philosopher who talks thus? But this affected sophist was of an amorous disposition.

be unwilling to survive you, and whose happiness depends on yours, do you think that you have no obligations to her? Will not the execution of your wicked design disturb the peace of a mind, which has been with much difficulty restored to its former innocence? Are not you afraid to add fresh torments to a heart of such sensibility? Are not you apprehensive lest your death should be attended with a loss more fatal, which would deprive the world and virtue itself of its brightest ornament? And if she should survive you, are not you afraid to rouse up remorse in her bosom, which is more grievous to support than life itself? Thou ungrateful friend! thou indelicate lover! Wilt thou always be taken up wholly with thyself? Wilt thou always think on thine own troubles alone? Hast thou no regard for the happiness of one who was so dear to thee? And cannot thou resolve to live for her who was willing to die with thee?

You talk of the duties of a magistrate, and of a father of a family; and because you

you are not under those circumstances, you think yourself absolutely free. And are you then under no obligations to society, to whom you are indebted for your preservation, your talents, your understanding? Do you owe nothing to your native country, and to those unhappy people who may need your existence! O what an accurate calculation you make! among the obligations you have enumerated, you have only omitted those of a man and of a citizen. Where is the virtuous patriot, who refused to enlist under a foreign prince, because his blood ought not to be spilt but in the service of his country; and who now, in a fit of despair, is ready to shed it against the express prohibition of the laws? The laws, the laws, young man! did any wise man ever despise them? Socrates, though innocent, out of regard to them refused to quit his prison. You do not scruple to violate them by quitting life unjustly; and you ask, what injury do I?

You endeavour to justify yourself by example. You presume to mention the Romans: You talk of the Romans! it becomes you indeed to cite those illustrious names! Tell me, did Brutus die a lover in despair, and did Cato plunge the dagger in his breast for his mistress? Thou weak and abject man! what resemblance is there between Cato and thee? Shew me the common standard between that sublime soul and thine. Ah! vain wretch! hold thy peace: I am afraid to profane his name by a vindication of his conduct. At that august and sacred name every friend of virtue should bow to the ground, and honour the memory of the greatest hero in silence.

How ill you have selected your examples, and how meanly you judge of the Romans, if you imagine that they thought themselves at liberty to quit life so soon as it became a burthen to them. Recur to the excellent days of that republic, and see whether you will find a single citizen of virtue, who thus freed himself from the discharge of his duty even after the most cruel misfortunes. When Regulus was on his return to Carthage, did he prevent the torments which he knew were preparing for him by destroying himself? What would not Posthumus have given, when obliged to pass under the yoke at Caudium, had this resource been justifiable? How much did even the senate admire that effort of courage, which enabled the consul Varro to survive his defeat? For what reason did so many generals voluntary surrender themselves to their enemies, they to whom ignominy was so dreadful, and who were so little afraid of dying? It was because they considered their blood, their life, and their latest breath, as devoted to their country; and neither shame nor misfortune could dissuade them from this sacred duty. But when the laws were subverted, and the state became a prey to tyranny, the citizens resumed their natural liberty, and the right they had over their own lives. When Rome was no more, it was lawful for the Romans to give up their lives; they had discharged their duties

ties on earth, they had no longer any country to defend, they were therefore at liberty to dispose of their lives, and to obtain that freedom for themselves which they could not recover for their country. After having spent their days in the service of expiring Rome, and in fighting for the defence of its laws, they died great and virtuous as they had lived, and their death was an additional tribute to the glory of the Roman name, since none of them beheld a sight above all others most dishonourable, that of a true citizen stooping to an usurper.

But thou, what art thou? What hast thou done? Dost thou think to excuse thyself on account of thy obscurity? Does thy weakness exempt thee from thy duty, and because thou hast neither rank nor distinction in thy country, art thou less subject to the laws? It becomes you vastly to presume to talk of dying, while you owe the service of your life to your equals. Know, that a death, such as you meditate, is shameful and surreptitious. It is a theft committed on mankind in general. Before you quit life, return the benefits you have received from every individual. But, say you, I have no attachments; I am useless in the world. O thou young philosopher! art thou ignorant that thou canst not move a single step without finding some duty to fulfil; and that every man is useful to society, even by means of his existence alone?

Hear me, thou rash young man! thou art dear to me. I commiserate thy errors. If the least sense of virtue still remains in thy breast, attend, and let me teach thee to be reconciled to life. Whenever thou art tempted to quit it, say to thyself——"Let me do at least one good action before I die." Then go in search for one in a state of indigence, whom thou mayest relieve; for one under misfortunes, whom thou mayest comfort; for one under oppression, whom thou mayest defend. Introduce to me those unhappy wretches, whom my rank keeps at a distance. Do not be afraid of misusing my purse, or my credit:

credit: make free with them; distribute my fortune; make me rich. If this consideration restrains you to-day, it will restrain you to-morrow; if to-morrow, it will restrain you all your life. If it has no power to restrain you, die! you are below my care.

# ON THE IMMORTALITY OF THE SOUL,
## AND A FUTURE STATE.

### By Mr. ADDISON.

THE courſe of my laſt ſpeculation led me inſenſibly into a ſubject, upon which I always meditate with great delight, I mean the immortality of the ſoul. I was yeſterday walking alone in one of my friend's woods, and loſt myſelf in it very agreeably, as I was running over in my mind the ſeveral arguments that eſtabliſh this great point, which is the baſis of morality, and the ſource of all the pleaſing hopes and ſecret joys that can ariſe in the heart of a reaſonable creature. I conſidered thoſe ſeveral proofs drawn,

First,

First, From the nature of the soul itself, and particularly its immateriality; which, though not absolutely necessary to the eternity of its duration, has, I think, been evinced to almost a demonstration.

Secondly, From its passions and sentiments, as particularly from its love of existence, its horror of annihilation, and its hopes of immortality, with that secret satisfaction which it finds in the practice of virtue, and that uneasiness which follows in it upon the commission of vice.

Thirdly, from the nature of the supreme Being, whose justice, goodness, wisdom and veracity, are all concerned in this great point.

But among these, and other excellent arguments for the immortality of the soul, there is one drawn from the perpetual progress of the soul to its perfection, without a possibility of ever arriving at it; which is a hint that I do not remember to have seen opened and improved by others who
have

have written on this subject, though it seems to me to carry a great weight with it. How can it enter into the thoughts of man, that the soul, which is capable of such immense perfections, and of receiving new improvements to all eternity, shall fall away into nothing almost as soon as it is created? Are such abilities made for no purpose? A brute arrives at a point of perfection that he can never pass: In a few years he has all the endowments he is capable of; and were he to live ten thousand more, would be the same thing he is at present. Were a human soul thus at a stand in her accomplishments, were her faculties to be full blown, and incapable of farther enlargements, I could imagine it might fall away insensibly, and drop at once into a state of annihilation. But can we believe a thinking being, that is in a perpetual progress of improvements, and travelling on from perfection to perfection, after having just looked abroad into the works of its Creator, and made a few discoveries of his infinite goodness, wisdom, and power, must perish at her first setting out,

out, and in the very beginning of her inquiries?

A man considered in his present state, seems only sent into the world to propagate his kind. He provides himself with a successor, and immediately quits his post to make room for him.

> ——— *Heires*
> *Hæredem alterius, velut unda supervenit undam.*
> Hor. lib. II. Epist. 2. v. 175.
>
> *Heir urges on his predecessor heir,*
> *Like wave impelling wave.*

He does not seem born to enjoy life, but to deliver it down to others. This is not surprising to consider in animals, which are formed for our use, and can finish their business in a short life. The silk-worm, after having spun her task, lays her eggs and dies. But a man can never have taken in his full measure of knowledge, has not time to subdue his passions, establish his soul in virtue, and come up to the perfection of his nature, before he is hurried off the stage. Would an infinitely wise Being make such glorious creatures for so mean a pura purpose? Can he delight in the production of such abortive intelligences, such short-lived reasonable beings? Would he give us talents that are not to be exerted? Capacities that are never to be gratified? How can we find that wisdom, which shines through all his works, in the formation of man, without looking on this world as only a nursery for the next, and believing that the several generations of rational creatures, which rise up and disappear in such quick successions, are only to receive their first rudiments of existence here, and afterwards to be transplanted into a more friendly climate, where they may spread and flourish to all eternity?

There is not, in my opinion, a more pleasing and triumphant consideration in religion than this, of the perpetual progress which the soul makes towards the perfection of its nature, without ever arriving at a period in it. To look upon the soul as going on from strength to strength, to consider that she is to shine for ever with new accessions of glory, and brighten to all eternity;

nity; that she will be still adding virtue to virtue, and knowledge to knowledge; carries in it something wonderfully agreeable to that ambition which is natural to the mind of man. Nay, it must be a prospect pleasing to God himself, to see his creation for ever beautifying in his eyes, and drawing nearer to him by greater degrees of resemblance.

Methinks this single consideration, of the progress of a finite spirit to perfection, will be sufficient to extinguish all envy in inferior natures, and all contempt in superior. That cherub, which now appears as a God to a human soul, knows very well, that the period will come about in eternity, when the human soul shall be as perfect as he himself now is: Nay, when she shall look down upon that degree of perfection, as much as she now falls short of it. It is true, the higher nature still advances, she by that means preserves his distance and superiority in the scale of being; but he knows, how high soever the station is, of which he stands possessed at present, the inferior nature will at length mount up to to it, and shine forth in the same degree of glory.

With what astonishment and veneration may we look into our own souls, where there are such hidden stores of virtue and knowledge, such inexhausted sources of perfection! We know not yet what we shall be, nor will it ever enter into the heart of man to conceive the glory that will be always in reserve for him. The soul considered with its Creator, is like one of those mathematical lines, that may draw nearer to another for all eternity, without a possibility of touching it: And can there be a thought so transporting, as to consider ourselves in these perpetual approaches to him, who is not only the standard of perfection, but of happiness!

I am fully persuaded, that one of the best springs of generous and worthy actions, is the having generous and worthy thoughts of ourselves. Whoever has a mean opinion of the dignity of his nature, will act in no higher a rank than he has
allotted

allotted himself in his own estimation. If he considers his being as circumscribed by the uncertain term of a few years, his designs will be contracted into the same narrow span he imagines is to bound his existance. How can he exalt his thoughts to any thing great and noble, who only believes, that, after a short turn on the stage of this world, he is to sink into oblivion, and to lose his consciousness for ever?

For this reason I am of opinion, that so useful and elevated a contemplation as that of the soul's immortality cannot be resumed too often. There is not a more improving exercise to the human mind, than to be frequently reviving its own great privileges and endowments; nor a more effectual means to awaken in us an ambition raised above low objects and little pursuits, than to value ourselves as heirs of eternity.

It is a very great satisfaction to consider the best and wisest of mankind, in all nations and ages, asserting, as with one voice,

M            this

this their birth-right, and to find it ratified by an express revelation. At the same time, if we turn our thoughts inward upon ourselves, we may meet with a kind of secret sense concurring with the proofs of our own immortality.

You have, ●●● opinion, raised a good presumptive ●●●ent from the increasing appetite the mind has to knowledge, and to the extending its own faculties, which cannot be accomplished, as the more restrained perfection of lower creatures may, in the limits of a short life. I think another probable conjecture may be raised from our appetite to duration itself, and from a reflexion on our progress through the several stages of it: we are complaining, as you observe in a former speculation, of the shortness of life, and yet are perpetually hurrying over the parts of it to arrive at certain little settlements, or imaginary points of rest, which are dispersed up and down in it.

Now

Now let us consider what happens to us, when we arrive at these imaginary points of rest: Do we stop our motion, and sit down satisfied in the settlement we have gained? or are we not removing the boundary, and marking out new points of rest, to which we press forward with the like eagerness, and which cease to be such as fast as we attain them? Our case is like that of a traveller upon the Alps, who should fancy that the top of the next hill must end his journey, because it terminates his prospect; but he no sooner arrives at it, than he sees new ground and other hills beyond it, and continues to travel on, as before.

This is so plainly every man's condition in life, that there is no one who has observed any thing, but may observe, that as fast as his time wears away, his appetite to something future remains. The use therefore I would make of it, is this; That since nature (as some love to express it) does nothing in vain, or to speak properly,

since

since the Author of our being has planted no wandering passion in it, no desire which has not its object, futurity is the proper object of the passion so constantly exercised about it; and this restlessness in the present, this assigning ourselves over to farther stages of duration, this successive grasping at somewhat still to come, appears to me (whatever it may to others) as a kind of instinct or natural symptom which the mind of man has of its own immortality.

I take it at the same time for granted, that the immortality of the soul is sufficiently established by other arguments: and if so, this appetite, which otherwise would be very unaccountable and absurd, seems very reasonable, and adds strength to the conclusion. But I am amazed, when I consider there are creatures capable of thought, who, in spite of every argument, can form to themselves a sullen satisfaction in thinking otherwise. There is something so pitifully mean in the inverted ambition,

bition of that man who can hope for annihilation, and please himself to think, that his whole fabric shall one day crumble into dust, and mix with the mass of inanimate beings, that it equally deserves our admiration and pity. The mystery of such mens unbelief is not hard to be penetrated; and indeed amounts to nothing more than a sordid hope that they shall not be immortal, because they dare not be so.

This brings me back to my first observation, and gives me occasion to say further, that as worthy actions spring from worthy thoughts, so worthy thoughts are likewise the consequence of worthy actions: But the wretch who has degraded himself below the character of immortality is very willing to resign his pretensions to it, and to substitute, in its room, a dark negative happiness in the extinction of his being.

The admirable Shakespeare has given us a very strong image of the unsupported condition of such a person in his last minutes,

nutes, in the second part of King Henry VI. where Cardinal Beaufort, who had been concerned in the murder of the good Duke Humphrey, is represented on his deathbed. After some short confused speeches which shew an imagination disturbed with guilt, just as he is expiring, King Henry standing by him, full of compassion, says,

> *Lord Cardinal! if thou thinkest on heaven's bliss,*
> *Hold up thy hand, make signal of that hope!*
> *He dies, and makes no sign!—*

The despair which is here shewn, without a word or action on the part of the dying person, is beyond what could be painted by the most forcible expressions whatever.

I shall not pursue this thought further, but only add, that as annihilation is not to be had with a wish, so it is the most abject thing in the world to wish it. What are honour, fame, wealth, or power, when compared with the generous expectation of a being without end, and a happiness adequate to that being?

The

The time present seldom affords sufficient employment to the mind of man. Objects of pain or pleasure, love or admiration, do not lay thick enough together in life to keep the soul in constant action, and supply an immediate exercise to its faculties. In order, therefore, to remedy this defect, that the mind may not want business, but always have materials for thinking, she is endued with certain powers, that can recal what is passed, and anticipate what is to come.

That wonderful faculty, which we call the memory, is perpetually looking back, when we have nothing present to entertain us. It is like those repositories in several animals, that are filled with stores of their former food, on which they may ruminate when their present pasture fails.

As the memory relieves the mind in her vacant moments, and prevents any chasms of thought by ideas of what is past, we have other faculties that agitate and employ her

her upon what is to come. These are the passions of *hope* and *fear*.

By these two passions we reach forward into futurity, and bring up to our present thoughts, objects that lie hid in the remotest depths of time. We suffer misery, and enjoy happiness before they are in being; we can set the sun and stars forward, or lose sight of them by wandering into those retired parts of eternity, when the heavens and earth shall be no more.

By the way; who can imagine that the existence of a creature is to be circumscribed by time, whose thoughts are not? But I shall, in this paper, confine myself to that particular passion which goes by the name of *hope*.

Our actual enjoyments are so few and transient, that man would be a very miserable being, were he not endued with this passion, which gives him a taste of those good things that may possibly come into

his

his poffeffion. "We fhould hope for every thing that is good, fays the old poet Linus, becaufe there is nothing which may not be hoped for, and nothing but what the gods are able to give us." Hope quickens all the ftill parts of life, and keeps the mind awake in her moft remifs and indolent hours. It gives habitual ferenity and good humour. It is a kind of vital heat in the foul, that cheers and gladdens her, when fhe does not attend to it. It makes pain eafy, and labour pleafant.

Befide thefe feveral advantages which rife from hope, there is another which is none of the leaft, and that is, its great efficacy in preferving us from fetting too high a value on prefent enjoyments. The faying of Cæfar is very well known. When he had given away all his eftate in gratuities among his friends, one of them afked, what he had left for himfelf? to which that great man replied, Hope. His natural magnanimity hindered him from prizing what he was certainly poffeffed of, and
turned

turned all his thoughts upon something more valuable that he had in view. I question not but every reader will draw a moral from this story, and apply it to himself without my direction.

The old story of Pandora's box, (which many of the learned believe was formed among the Heathens, upon the tradition of the fall of man) shews us how deplorable a state they thought the present life, without hope. To set forth the utmost condition of misery, they tell us, that our forefathers, according to the Pagan theology, had a great vessel presented him by Pandora: Upon his lifting up the lid of it, says the fable, there flew out all the calamities and distempers incident to men, from which, till that time, they had been altogether exempt. Hope, who had been inclosed in the cup with so much bad company, instead of flying off with the rest, stuck so close to the lid of it, that it was shut down upon her.

I shall

I shall make but two reflections upon what I have hitherto said. First, that no kind of life is so happy as that which is full of hope, especially when the hope is well grounded, and when the object of it is of an exalted kind, and in its nature proper to make the person happy who enjoys it. This proposition must be very evident to those who consider how few are the present enjoyments of the most happy man, and how insufficient to give him an entire satisfaction and acquiescence in them.

My next observation is this, that a religious life is that which most abounds in a well-grounded hope, and such an one as is fixed on objects that are capable of making us entirely happy. This Hope in a religious man, is much more sure and certain than the hope of any temporal blessing, as it is strengthened not only by reason, but by faith. It has at the same time its eye perpetually fixed on that state, which implies, in the very notion of it, the most full and the most compleat happiness.

I have

I have before shewn how the influence of hope in general sweetens life, and makes our present condition supportable, if not pleasing; but a religious hope has still greater advantages. It does not only bear up the mind under her sufferings, but makes her rejoice in them, as they may be the instruments of procuring her the great and ultimate end of all her hope.

Religious hope has likewise this advantage above any other kind of hope, that it is able to revive the dying man, and to fill his mind not only with secret comfort and refreshment, but sometimes with rapture and transport. He triumphs in his agonies, whilst the soul springs forward with delight to the great object which she has always had in view, and leaves the body with an expectation of being re-united to her in a glorious and joyful resurrection.

I shall conclude this essay with those emphatical expressions of a lively hope, which the Psalmist made use of in the midst of
those

those dangers and adversities which surrounded him; for the following passage had its present and personal, as well as its future and prophetic sense. "I have set the Lord always before me: because he is at my right hand I shall not be moved. Therefore my heart is glad, and my glory rejoiceth: my flesh also shall rest in hope. For thou wilt not leave my soul in hell, neither wilt thou suffer thine holy one to see corruption. Thou wilt shew me the path of life: in thy presence is fulness of joy, at thy right hand there are pleasures for evermore."

———

It has been usual to remind persons of rank, on great occasions in life, of their race and quality, and to what expectations they were born; that, by considering what is worthy of them, they may be withdrawn from mean pursuits, and encouraged to laudable undertakings. This is turning nobility into a principle of virtue, and making it productive of merit, as it is understood

derstood to have been originally a reward of ſin.

It is for the like reaſon, I imagine, that you have in ſome of your ſpeculations, aſſerted to your readers the dignity of human nature. But you cannot be inſenſible that this is a controverted doctrine; there are authors who conſider human nature in a very different view, and books of maxims have been written to ſhew the falſity of all human virtues. The reflexions which are made on this ſubject uſually take ſome tincture from the tempers and characters of thoſe who make them. Politicians can reſolve the moſt ſhining actions among men into artifice and deſign; others, who are ſoured by diſcontent, repulſes, or ill uſage, are apt to miſtake their ſpleen for philoſophy; men of profligate lives, and ſuch as find themſelves incapable of riſing to any diſtinction among their fellow creatures, are for pulling down all appearances of merit, which ſeem to upbraid them: and Satiriſts deſcribe nothing but deformity.

From

From all these hands we have such draughts of mankind as are represented in those burlesque pictures, which the Italians call Caracaturas; where the art consists in preserving, amidst distorted proportions and aggravated features, some distinguishing likeness of the person, but in such a manner as to transform the most agreeable beauty into the most odious monster.

It is very disingenuous to level the best of mankind with the worst, and for the faults of particulars to degrade the whole species. Such methods tend not only to remove a man's good opinion of others, but to destroy that reverence for himself, which is a great guard of innocence, and a spring of virtue.

It is true indeed, that there are surprising mixtures of beauty and deformity, of wisdom and folly, virtue and vice in the human make; such a disparity is found among numbers of the same kind, and every individual, in some instances, or at

some

sometimes, is so unequal to himself, that man seems to be the most wavering and inconsistent being in the whole creation. So that the question in morality, concerning the dignity of our nature, may at first sight appear like some difficult questions in Natural Philosophy, in which the arguments on both sides seem to be of equal strength. But as I began with considering this point, as it relates to action, I shall here borrow an admirable reflexion from Monsieur Pascal, which I think sets it in its proper light.

It is of dangerous consequence, says he, to represent to man how near he is to the level of beasts, without shewing him at the same time his greatness. It is likewise dangerous to let him see his greatness without his meanness. It is more dangerous yet to leave him ignorant of either; but very beneficial that he should be made sensible of both. Whatever imperfections we may have in our nature, it is the business of religion and virtue to rectify them

them, as far as is consistent with our present state. In the mean time, it is no small encouragement to generous minds to consider that we shall put them all off with our mortality. That sublime manner of salutation with which the Jews approached their kings,

*O King, live for ever!*

may be addressed to the lowest and most despised mortal among us, under all the infirmities and distresses with which we see him surrounded. And whoever believes the immortality of the soul, will not need a better argument for the dignity of his nature, nor a stronger incitement to actions suitable to it.

I am naturally led by this reflexion to a subject I have already touched upon in a former letter, and cannot without pleasure call to mind the thoughts of Cicero to this purpose, in the close of his book concerning old age. Every one who is acquainted with his writings will remember, that the elder Cato is introduced in that discourse as the speaker; and Scipio and Lelius are his auditors. This venerable person is represented looking forward as it were from the verge of extreme old age, into a future state, and rising into a contemplation on the unperishable part of his nature, and its existence after death. I shall collect part of his discourse; and, as you have formerly offered some arguments for the soul's immortality, agreeable both to reason and the Christian doctrine, I believe your readers will not be displeased to see how the same great truth shines in the pomp of Roman eloquence.

"This, says Cato, is my firm persuasion, that since the human soul exerts itself with so great activity, since it has such a remembrance of the past, such a concern for the future, since it is enriched with so many arts, sciences and discoveries, it is impossible but the being which contains all these must be immortal."

The elder Cyrus, just before his death,

is represented by Xenophon speaking after this manner: "Think not, my dearest children, that when I depart from you, I shall be no more, but remember, that my soul, even while I lived among you, was invisible to you; yet by my actions you were sensible it existed in this body. Believe it therefore existing still, though it be still unseen. How quickly would the honours of illustrious men perish after death, if their souls performed nothing to preserve their fame? For my own part, I could never think that the soul, while in a mortal body, lives; or when departed out of it, dies; or that its consciousness is lost when it is discharged out of an unconscious habitation. But when it is freed from all corporeal alliance, then it truly exists. Further, since the human frame is broken by death, tell us what becomes of its parts? It is visible whither the materials of other beings are translated, namely, to the source from whence they had their birth. The soul alone, neither present nor departed, is the object of our eyes."

Thus

Thus Cyrus. But to proceed. No one shall persuade me, Scipio, that your worthy father, or your grandfathers, Paulus and and Africanus, or Africanus his father, or uncle, or many other excellent men whom I need not name, performed so many actions to be remembered by posterity, without being sensible that futurity was their right. And, if I may be allowed an old man's privilege, to speak of myself, do you think I would have endured the fatigue of so many wearisome days and nights both at home and abroad, if I imagined that the same boundary which is set to my life must terminate my glory? Were it not more desirable to have worn out my days in ease and tranquillity, free from labour, and without emulation? But I know not how, my soul has always raised itself, and looked forward on futurity, in this view and expectation, that when it shall depart out of life, it shall then live for ever: and if this were not true, that the mind is immortal, the souls of the most worthy would not, above all others, have the strongest impulse to glory.

What

What besides this is the cause that the wisest men die with the greatest equanimity, the ignorant with the greatest concern? Does it not seem, that those minds which have the most extensive views, foresee they are removing to a happier condition, which those of a narrow sight do not perceive? I, for my part, am transported with the hope of seeing your ancestors, whom I have honoured and loved, and am earnestly desirous of meeting not only those excellent persons whom I have known, but those too of whom I have heard and read, and of whom I myself have written; nor would I be detained from so pleasing a journey. O happy day! when I shall escape from this croud, this heap of pollution, and be admitted to that divine assembly of exalted spirits! when I shall go not only to those great persons I have named, but to my Cato, my son, than whom a better man was never born, and whose funeral rites I myself performed; whereas he ought rather to have attended mine. Yet has not his soul deserted me, but seeming

to

to cast back a look on me, is gone before to those habitations to which it was sensible I should follow him. And though I might appear to have borne my loss with courage, I was not unaffected with it; but I comforted myself in the assurance that it would not be long before we should meet again, and be divorced no more.

---

A lewd young fellow seeing an aged hermit go by him bare-foot, "Father, says he, you are in a very miserable condition, if there is not another world. True, son, said the hermit; but what is thy condition if there is?" Man is a creature designed for two different states of being, or rather for two different lives. His first life is short and transient; his second permanent and lasting. The question we are all concerned in, is this; In which of these two lives it is our chief interest to make ourselves happy? Or in other words, Whether we should endeavour to secure to ourselves
the

the pleasures and gratifications of a life which is uncertain and precarious, and at its utmost length, of a very inconsiderable duration; or to secure to ourselves the pleasures of a life which is fixed and settled, and will never end? Every man, upon the first hearing of this question, knows very well which side of it he ought to close with. But however right we are in theory, it is plain, that in practice we adhere to the wrong side of the question. We make provisions for this life as though it were never to have an end, and for the other life as though it were never to have a beginning.

Should a spirit of superior rank, who is a stranger to human nature, accidentally alight upon the earth, and take a survey of its inhabitants; what would his notions of us be? Would not he think that we are a species of beings made for quite different ends and purposes than what we really are? Must not he imagine that we were placed in this world to get riches and honours?

honours? Would not he think that it was our duty to toil after wealth, and station, and title? Nay, would not he believe we were forbidden poverty by threats of eternal punishment, and enjoined to pursue our pleasures under pain of damnation? He would certainly imagine that we were influenced by a scheme of duties quite opposite to those which are indeed prescribed to us. And truly, according to such an imagination, he must conclude that we are a species of the most obedient creatures in the universe; that we are constant to our duty; and that we keep a steady eye on the end for which we were sent hither.

But how great would be his astonishment, when he learned that we were beings not designed to exist in this world above threescore and ten years? and that the greatest part of this busy species fall short even of that age? How would he be lost in horror and admiration, when he should know that this set of creatures, who lay out all their endeavours for this life, which

scarce

scarce deserves the name of existence, when, I say, he should know that this set of creatures are to exist to all eternity in another life, for which they make no preparations? Nothing can be a greater disgrace to reason, than that men, who are persuaded of these two different states of being, should be perpetually employed in providing for a life of threescore and ten years, and neglecting to make provision for that, which after many myriads of years will be still new, and still beginning; especially when we consider that our endeavours for making ourselves great, or rich, or honourable, or whatever else we place our happiness in, may after all prove unsuccessful; whereas, if we constantly and sincerely endeavour to make ourselves happy in the other life, we are sure that our endeavours will succeed, and that we shall not be disappointed of our hope.

The following question is started by one of the schoolmen. Supposing the whole body of the earth were a great ball or mass of the finest sand, and that a single grain or particle of this sand should be annihilated every thousand years. Supposing then that you had it in your choice to be happy all the while this prodigious mass of sand was consuming by this slow method till there was not a grain of it left, on condition you were to be miserable for ever after; or supposing that you might be happy for ever after, on condition you would be miserable till the whole mass of sand were thus annihilated at the rate of one sand in a thousand years: Which of these two cases would you make your choice?

It must be confessed in this case, so many thousands of years are to the imagination as a kind of eternity, though in reality they do not bear so great a proportion to that duration which is to follow them, as an unit does to the greatest number which you can put together in figures, or as one of those sands to the supposed heap. Reason therefore tells us, without any manner of of hesitation, which would be the better part in this choice. However, as I have before intimated, our reason might in such case be so overset by the imagination, as to dispose some persons to sink under the consideration of the great length of the first part of this duration, and of the great distance of that second duration which is to succeed it. The mind, I say, might give itself up to that happiness which is at hand, considering that it is so very near, and that it would last so very long. But when the choice we actually have before us, is this, Whether we will chuse to be happy for the space only of threescore and ten, nay, perhaps of only twenty or ten years, I might say of only a day or an hour, and miserable to all eternity: or, on the contrary, miserable for this short term of years, and happy for a whole eternity: What words are sufficient to express that folly and want of consideration, which in such a case makes a wrong choice?

I here put the case even at the worst, by

supposing, what seldom happens, that a course of virtue makes us miserable in this life: But if we suppose, as it generally happens, that virtue would make us more happy even in this life, than a contrary course of vice; how can we sufficiently admire the stupidity or madness of those persons who are capable of making so absurd a choice?

Every wise man therefore will consider this life only as it may conduce to the happiness of the other, and cheerfully sacrifice the pleasures of a few years to those of an eternity.

---

IF the universe be the creature of an intelligent mind, this mind could have no immediate regard to himself in producing it. He needed not to make trial of his omnipotence, to be informed what effects were within its reach: The world, as existing in his eternal idea, was then as beautiful

tiful as now it is drawn forth into being; and in the immense abyss of his essence are contained far brighter scenes than will be ever set forth to view; it being impossible that the great author of nature should bound his own power by giving existence to a system of creatures so perfect, that he cannot improve upon it by any other exertions of his almighty will. Between finite and infinite there is an unmeasured interval, not to be filled up in endless ages; for which reason the most excellent of all God's works must be equally short of what his power is able to produce as the most imperfect, and may be exceeded with the same ease.

This thought hath made some imagine, (what, it must be confessed, is not impossible,) that the unfathomed space is ever teeming with new births, the younger still inheriting a greater perfection than the elder. But as this doth not fall within my present view, I shall content myself with taking notice, that the consideration now mentioned proves undeniably, that the ideal worlds in the divine understanding yield a prospect incomparably more ample, various and delightful than any created world can do: And that therefore, as it is not to be supposed that God should make a world merely of inanimate matter, however diversified; or inhabited only by creatures of no higher an order than brutes; so the end for which he designed his reasonable offspring, is the contemplation of his works, the enjoyment of himself, and in both to be happy, having, to this purpose, endued them with correspondent faculties and desires. He can have no greater pleasure from a bare review of his works, than from the survey of his own ideas; but we may be assured that he is well pleased in the satisfaction derived to beings capable of it, and for whose entertainment he hath erected this immense theatre. Is not this more than an intimation of our immortality? Man, who when considered as on his probation for a happy existence hereafter,

is

is the moſt remarkable inſtance of divine wiſdom; if we cut him off from all relation to eternity, is the moſt wonderful and unaccountable compoſition in the whole creation. He hath capacities to lodge a much greater variety of knowledge than he will be ever maſter of, and an unſatisfied curioſity to tread the ſecret paths of nature and providence; but, with this, his organs, in their preſent ſtructure, are rather fitted to ſerve the neceſſities of a vile body, than to miniſter to his underſtanding; and, from the little ſpot to which he is chained, he can frame but wandering gueſſes concerning the innumerable worlds of light that encompaſs him, which, though in themſelves of a prodigious bigneſs, do but juſt glimmer in the remote ſpaces of the heavens; and when, with a great deal of time and pains, he hath laboured a little way up the ſteep aſcent of truth, and beholds with pity the groveling multitude beneath, in a moment his foot ſlides, and he tumbles down headlong into the grave.

Thinking on this, I am obliged to believe, in justice to the Creator of the world, that there is another state when man shall be better situated for contemplation, or rather have it in his power to remove from object to object, and from world to world; and be accomodated with senses, and other helps, for making the quickest and most amazing discoveries. How does such a genius as Sir Isaac Newton, from amidst the darkness that involves human understanding, break forth, and appear like one of another species! The vast machine we inhabit, lies open to him, he seems not unacquainted with the general laws that govern it; and while with the transport of a philosopher he beholds and admires the glorious work, he is capable of paying at once a more devout and more rational homage to his Maker. But alas! how narrow is the prospect even of such a mind? and how obscure to the compass that is taken in by the ken of an angel; or of a soul but newly escaped from its imprisonment in the body! For my part, I freely
indulge

indulge my soul in the confidence of its future grandeur; it pleases me to think that I, who know so small a portion of the works of the Creator, and with slow and painful steps creep up and down on the surface of this globe, shall ere long shoot away with the swiftness of imagination, trace out the hidden springs of nature's operation, be able to keep pace with the heavenly bodies in the rapidity of their career, be a spectator of the long chain of events in the natural and moral worlds, visit the several apartments of the creation, know how they are furnished and how inhabited, comprehend the order, and measure the magnitudes and distances of those orbs, which to us seem disposed without any regular design, and set all in the same circle; observe the dependence of the parts of each system, and, if our minds are big enough to grasp the theory of the several systems upon one another, from whence results the harmony of the universe. In eternity a great deal may be done of this kind. I find it of use to cherish this generous

ous ambition; for besides the secret refreshment it diffuses through my soul, it engages me in an endeavour to improve my faculties, as well as to exercise them conformably to the rank I now hold among reasonable beings, and the hope I have of being once advanced to a more exalted station.

The other, and that the ultimate end of man, is the enjoyment of God, beyond which he cannot form a wish. Dim at best are the conceptions we have of the supreme Being, who, as it were, keeps his creatures in suspence, neither discovering, nor hiding himself; by which means the libertine hath a handle to dispute his existence, while the most are content to speak him fair, but in their hearts prefer every trifling satisfaction to the favour of their Maker, and ridicule the good man for the singularity of his choice. Will there not a time come, when a Free-thinker shall see his impious schemes overturned, and be made a convert to the truths he hates;

hates; when deluded mortals shall be convinced of the folly of their pursuits, and the few wise who followed the guidance of heaven, and, scorning the blandishments of sense and the sordid bribery of the world, aspired to a celestial abode, shall stand possessed of their utmost wish in the vision of the Creator? Here the mind heaves a thought now and then towards him, and hath some transient glances of his presence: When in the instant it thinks itself to have the fastest hold, the object eludes its expectations, and it falls back tired and baffled to the ground. Doubtless there is some more perfect way of conversing with heavenly beings. Are not spirits capable of mutual intelligence, unless immersed in bodies, or by their intervention? Must superior natures depend on inferior for the main privilege of sociable beings, that of conversing with, and knowing each other? What would they have done, had matter never been created? I suppose, not have lived in eternal solitude. As incorporeal substances are of a nobler

order,

order, so, be sure, their manner of intercourse is answerably more expedite and intimate. This method of communication we call intellectual vision, as somewhat analogous to the sense of seeing, which is the medium of our acquaintance with this visible world. And in some such way can God make himself the object of immediate intuition to the blessed; and as he can, it is not improbable that he will, always condescending, in the circumstances of doing it, to the weakness and proportion of finite minds. His works but faintly reflect the image of his perfections, it is a second-hand knowledge: To have a just idea of him, it may be necessary that we see him as he is. But what is that? It is something that never entered into the heart of man to conceive; yet, what we can easily conceive, will be a fountain of unspeakable, of everlasting rapture. All created glories will fade and die away in his presence. Perhaps it will be my happiness to compare the world with the fair exemplar of it in the divine mind; perhaps to view the original plan of those wise designs that have been executing in a long succession of ages. Thus employed in finding out his works, and contemplating their author, how shall I fall prostrate and adoring, my body swallowed up in the immensity of matter, my mind in the infinitude of his perfections!

---

In compassion to those gloomy mortals, who by their unbelief are rendered incapable of feeling those impressions of joy and hope, which the celebration of the glorious Easter festival naturally leaves on the mind of a Christian, I shall endeavour to evince, that there are grounds to expect a future state, without supposing in the reader any faith at all, not even the belief of a Deity. Let the most stedfast unbeliever open his eyes, and take a survey of the sensible world, and then say if there be not a connexion and adjustment

justment, an exact and constant order discoverable in all the parts of it. Whatever be the cause, the thing itself is evident to all our faculties. Look into the animal system, the passions, senses, and locomotive powers; is not the like contrivance and propriety observable in these too? Are they not fitted to certain ends, and are they not by nature directed to proper objects?

Is it possible then that the smallest bodies should, by a management superior to the wit of man, be disposed in the most excellent manner agreeable to their respective natures; and yet the spirits or souls of men be neglected, or managed by such rules as fall short of man's understanding? Shall every other passion be rightly placed by nature, and shall that appetite of immortality natural to all mankind be alone misplaced, or designed to be frustrated? Shall the industrious application of the inferior animal powers in the meanest vocations be answered by the ends we we propose, and shall not the generous efforts of a virtuous mind be rewarded? In a word, shall the corporeal world be all order and harmony, the intellectual discord and confusion? He, who is bigot enough to believe these things, must bid adieu to that natural rule of reasoning from analogy; must run counter to that maxim of common sense, "That men ought to form their judgment of things unexperienced from what they have experienced."

If any thing looks like a recompence of calamitous virtue on this side the grave, it is either an assurance that thereby we obtain the favour and protection of Heaven, and shall, whatever befals us in this, in another life meet with a just return; or else that applause and reputation, which is thought to attend virtuous actions. The former of these, our Free-thinkers, out of their singular wisdom and benevolence to mankind, endeavour to erase from the minds of men. The latter can never be justly distributed in this life, where so many ill actions are reputable, and so many good actions disesteemed or misinterpreted; where subtle hypocrisy is placed in the most engaging light, and modest virtue lies concealed; where the heart and the soul are hid from the eyes of men, and the eyes of men are dimmed and vitiated. Plato's sense in relation to this point is contained in his Gorgias, where he introduces Socrates speaking after this manner.

"It was in the reign of Saturn provided by a law, which the gods have since continued down to this time, That they who have lived virtuously and piously upon earth, should after death enjoy a life full of happiness, in certain islands appointed for the habitation of the blessed: but that such as had lived wickedly should go into the receptacle of damned souls, named Tartarus, there to suffer the punishments they deserved. But in all the reign of Saturn, and in the beginning of the reign of Jove, living judges were appointed, by whom each person was judged in his lifetime,

time, in the same day on which he was to die. The consequence of which was, that they often passed wrong judgments. Pluto, therefore, who presided in Tartarus, and the guardians of the blessed islands, finding that, on the other side, many unfit persons were sent to their respective dominions, complained to Jove, who promised to redress the evil. He added, the reason of these unjust proceedings is that men are judged in the body. Hence many conceal the blemishes and imperfections of their minds by beauty, birth and riches: not to mention, that at the time of trial, there are crouds of witnesses to attest their having lived well. These things mislead the judges, who being themselves also of the number of the living are surrounded each with his body, as with a veil thrown over his mind. For the future, therefore, it is my intention that men do not come on their trial till after death, when they shall appear before the judge, disrobed of all their corporeal ornaments. The judge himself too shall be a pure unveiled spirit, beholding

the

the very soul, the naked soul, of the party before him. With this view, I have already constituted my sons, Minos and Rhadamanthus, judges, who are natives of Asia, and Æacus, a native of Europe. These after death, shall hold their court in a certain meadow, from which there are two roads, leading the one to Tartarus, the other to the islands of the blessed."

From this, as from numberless other passages of his writings, may be seen Plato's opinion of a future state. A thing therefore in regard to us so comfortable, in itself so just and excellent, a thing so agreeable to the analogy of nature, and so universally credited by all orders and ranks of men, of all nations and ages, what is it that should move a few men to reject? Surely there must be something of prejudice in the case. I appeal to the secret thoughts of a Freethinker, if he does not argue within himself after this manner: The senses and faculties I enjoy at present are visibly designed to repair, or preserve the body from

the

the injuries it is liable to in its present circumstances. But in an eternal state, where no decays are to be repaired, no outward injuries to be fenced against, where there are no flesh and bones, nerves or blood-vessels, there will certainly be none of the senses. And that there should be a state of life without the senses is inconceivable.

But as this manner of reasoning proceeds from a poverty of imagination, and narrowness of soul in those who use it, I shall endeavour to remedy those defects, and open their views, by laying before them a case which, being naturally possible, may perhaps reconcile them to the belief of what is supernaturally revealed.

Let us suppose a man blind and deaf from his birth, who being grown to man's estate, is by the dead palsy, or by some other case, deprived of his feeling, tasting, and smelling; and at the same time has the impediment of his hearing removed, and the film taken away from his eyes:
what

what the five senses are to us, that the touch, taste, and smell were to him. And any other ways of perception of a more refined and extensive nature were to him as inconceivable, as to us those are, which will one day be adapted to perceive those things which "eye hath not seen, nor ear heard, neither hath it entered into the heart of man to conceive." And it would be just as reasonable in him to conclude, that the loss of those three senses could not possibly be succeeded by any new inlets of perception; as in a modern Free-thinker to imagine there can be no state of life and perception without the senses he enjoys at present. Let us further suppose the same person's eyes, at their first opening, to be struck with a great variety of the most gay and pleasing objects, and his ears with a melodious concert of vocal and instrumental music: behold him amazed, ravished, transported; and you have some distant representation, some faint and glimmering idea of the ecstatic state of the soul in that article in which she emerges from
this

this sepulchre of flesh into life and immortality.

---

There are no speculations which please me more than those upon infinitude and eternity. I have already considered that part of eternity which is past, and wish to give my thoughts upon that which is to come.

This view of eternity will afford infinitely greater pleasure than the former, since we have every one of us a concern in that which is to come: whereas a speculation on that which is past is rather curious than useful.

Besides, we can easily conceive it possible for successive duration never to have an end; though I have observed, that eternity which never had a beginning is altogether incomprehensible; that is, we can conceive an eternal duration which may be, though we cannot an eternal duration which hath been;

been; or, if I may use the philosophical terms, we may apprehend a potential though not an actual eternity.

This notion of a future eternity, which is natural to the mind of man, is an unanswerable argument that he is a being designed for it: especially if we consider that he is capable of being virtuous or vicious here; that he hath faculties improvable to all eternity; and by a proper or wrong employment of them, may be happy or miserable throughout that infinite duration. Our idea indeed of this eternity is not of an adequate or fixed nature, but is perpetually growing and enlarging itself toward the object, which is too big for human comprehension. As we are not in the beginning of existence, so shall we always appear to ourselves as if we were for ever entering upon it. After a million or two of centuries, some considerable things already past, may slip out of our memory: which, if it be not strengthened in a wonderful manner, may possibly forget that ever there was a

sun

sun or planets. And yet notwithstanding the long race that we shall then have run, we shall still imagine ourselves just starting from the goal, and find no proportion between that space which we know had a beginning, and what we are sure will never have an end.

Here follows a translation of the speech of Cato on this occasion, which for concifeness, purity, and elegance of phrase cannot be sufficiently admired."

## ACT V. SCEN. I.

### CATO *solus, &c.*

*SIC, sic se habere rem necesse prorsus est,*
  *Ratione vincis, do lubens manus, Plato.*
*Quid enim dedisset, Quae dedit frustra nihil,*
*Aeternitatis insitam cupidinem*
*Natura? Quorsum haec dulcis-expectatio;*
*Vitaeque non explenda melioris sitis?*
*Quid vult sibi aliud iste redeundi in nihil*
*Horror, sub imis quemque agens praecordiis?*
*Cur territa in se refugit anima, cur tremit*
*Attonita, quatiens, morte ne pereat, timet?*
*Particula nempe est cuique nascenti indita*
*Divinior; quae corpus incolens agit;*
*Hominique succinit, sua est Aeternitas.*
*Aeternitas! O lubricum nimis aspici,*
*Mixtumque dulci gaudium formidine!*

  *Quae demigrabitur alia hinc in corpora?*
*Quae terra mox incognita? Quis orbis novus,*
*Manet incolendus? Quanta erit mutatio?*
*Haec intuenti spatia mihi quaqua patent*
*Immensa; sed caliginosa nox premit;*
*Nec luce clara vult videri singula.*
*Figendus hic pes; certa sunt haec hactenus:*
*Si quod gubernet numen humanum genus,*
*(At, quod gubernet, esse clamant omnia)*
*Virtute non gaudere certe non potest:*
*Nec esse non beata, qua gaudet potest.*
*Sed qua beata sede? Quove in tempore?*
*Haec quanta quanta terra, tota est Caesaris.*
*Quid dubius haeret animus usque adeo? Brevi*
*Hic nodum hic omnem expediet.    Arma en induor,*
                    [*Ensi manum admovens,*

*In*

## ACT V. SCENE I.

CATO alone, &c.

IT must be so—*Plato*, thou reason'st well—
Else whence this pleasing hope, this fond desire,
This longer after immortality?
Or whence this secret dread, and inward horror,
Of falling into nought? Why shrinks the soul
Back on herself, and startles at destruction?
'Tis the divinity that stirs within us;
'Tis heav'n itself, that points out an hereafter,
And intimates eternity to man.
Eternity! thou pleasing, dreadful, thought!

Through what variety of untry'd being,
Through what new scenes and changes must we pass!
The wide, th' unbounded prospect, lies before me;
But shadows, clouds, and darkness rest upon it.
Here will I hold. If there's a pow'r above us,
(And that there is, all nature cries aloud
Through all her works) He must delight in virtue;
And that which he delights in must be happy.
But when! or where!—This world was made for *Cæsar*;
'm weary of conjectures—This must end 'em.
[*Laying his hand on his sword.*
Thus

*In utramque partem facta; quaeque vim inferant,*
*Et quae propulsent! Dextera intentat necem;*
*Vitam sinistra: vulnus haec dabit manus;*
*Altera medelam vulneris: hic ad exitum*
*Deducet, ictu simplici; haec vetant mori.*
*Secura ridet anima mucronis minas,*
*Ensesque strictas, interire nescia.*
*Extinguet aetas sidera diuturnior:*
*Aetate languens ipse sol obscurius*
*Emittet orbi consenescenti jubar:*
*Natura et ipsa sentiet quondam vices*
*Aetates; annis ipsa deficiet gravis;*
*At tibi juventus, at tibi immortalitas;*
*Tibi parta divum est vita. Periment mutuis*
*Elementa sese et interibunt ictibus:*
*Tu permanebis sola semper integra,*
*Tu cuncta rerum quassa, cuncta naufraga,*
*Jam portu in ipso tuta, contemplabere.*
*Compage rupta, corruent in se invicem,*
*Orbesque fractis ingerentur orbibus;*
*Illaesa tu sedebis extra fragmina.*

Thus am I doubly arm'd; my death and life,
My bane and antidote, are both before me.
This in a moment brings me to an end;
But this informs me, I shall never die.
The soul, secur'd in her existence, smiles
At the drawn dagger, and defies its point.
The stars shall fade away, the sun himself
Grow dim with age, and nature sink in years;
But thou shalt flourish in immortal youth,
Unhurt amidst the war of elements,
The wrecks of matter, and the crush of worlds.

THE same faculty of reason and understanding, which placeth us above the brute part of the creation, doth also subject our minds to greater and more manifold disquiets than creatures of an inferior rank are sensible of. It is by this that we anticipate future disasters, and oft create to ourselves real pain from imaginary evils, as well as multiply the pangs arising from those which cannot be avoided.

It behoves us therefore to make the best use of that sublime talent, which, so long as it continues the instrument of passion, will serve only to make us more miserable, in proportion as we are more excellent than other beings.

It is the privilege of a thinking being to withdraw from the objects that solicit his senses, and turn his thoughts inward on himself. For my own part, I often mitigate the pain arising from the little misfortunes and disappointments that chequer human life by this introversion of my faculties,

culties, wherein I regard my own soul as the image of her Creator, and receive great consolation from beholding those perfections which testify her divine original, and lead me into some knowledge of her everlasting archetype.

But there is not any property or circumstance of my being that I contemplate with more joy than my immortality. I can easily overlook my present momentary sorrow, when I reflect that it is in my power to be happy a thousand years hence. If it were not for this thought, I had rather be an oyster than a man, the most stupid and senseless of animals than a reasonable mind tortured with an extreme innate desire of that perfection which it despairs to obtain.

It is with great pleasure that I behold instinct, reason, and faith concurring to attest this comfortable truth. It is revealed from heaven, it is discovered by philosophers, and the ignorant, unenlightened part of mankind

kind have a natural propensity to believe it. It is an agreeable entertainment to reflect on the various shapes under which this doctrine has appeared in the world. The Pythagorean transmigration, the sensual habitations of the Mahometan, and the shady realms of Pluto, do all agree in the main points, the continuation of our existence and the distribution of rewards and punishments, proportioned to the merits or demerits of men in this life.

But in all these schemes there is something gross and improbable, that shocks a reasonable and speculative mind. Whereas nothing can be more rational and sublime than the christian idea of a future state. "Eye hath not seen, nor ear heard, neither hath it entered into the heart of man to conceive the things which God hath prepared for those that love him." The above mentioned schemes are narrow transcripts of our present state: but in this indefinite description there is something ineffably great and noble. The mind of man must be be raised to a higher pitch, not only to partake the enjoyments of the Christian paradise, but even to be able to frame any notion of them.

Nevertheless, in order to gratify our imagination, and by way of condescension to our low way of thinking, the ideas of light, glory, a crown, &c. are made use of to adumbrate that which we cannot directly understand. "The Lamb which is in the midst of the throne shall feed them, and shall lead them into living fountains of waters; and God shall wipe away all tears from their eyes. And there shall be no more death, neither sorrow nor crying, neither shall there be any more pain; for the former things are passed away; and behold all things are new. There shall be no night there, and they need no candle, neither light of the sun: for the Lord God giveth them light, and shall make them drink of the river of his pleasures: and they shall reign for ever and ever. They shall receive

receive a crown of glory, which fadeth not away."

These are cheering reflections: and I have often wondered that men could be found so dull and phlegmatic, as to prefer the thought of annihilation before them; or so ill-natured, as to endeavour to persuade mankind to the disbelief of what is so pleasing and profitable even in the prospect; or so blind, as not to see that there is a Deity, and if there be, that this scheme of things flows from his attributes, and evidently corresponds with the other parts of his creation.

I know not how to account for this absurd turn of thought, except it proceed from a want of other employment, joined with an affectation of singularity. I shall, therefore, inform our modern Free-thinkers of two points, whereof they seem to be ignorant. The first is, that it is not the being singular, but being singular for something that argues either extraordinary endueendowments of nature, or benevolent intentions to mankind, which draws the admiration and esteem of the world. A mistake in this point naturally arises from that confusion of thought which I do not remember to have seen so great instances of in any writers, as in certain modern Free-thinkers.

The other point is, that there are innumerable objects within the reach of a human mind, and each of these objects may be viewed in innumerable lights and positions, and the relations arising between them are innumerable. There is, therefore, an infinity of things whereon to employ their thoughts, if not with advantage to the world, at least with amusement to themselves, and without offence or prejudice to other people. If they proceed to exert their talent of Free-thinking in this way, they may be innocently dull, and no one take any notice of it. But to see men without either wit or argument pretend to run down divine and human laws, and treat their fellow-subjects with contempt for pro-

fessing

fessing a belief of those points on which the present as well as future interest of mankind depends, is not to be endured. For my own part, I shall omit no endeavours to render their persons as despicable and their practices as odious, in the eye of the world, as they deserve.

I have already taken a particular pleasure in examining the opinions which men of different religions, different ages, and different countries have entertained concerning the immortality of the soul, and the state of happiness which they promise themselves in another world. For whatever prejudices and errors human nature lies under, we find that either reason or tradition from our first parents, has discovered to all people something in these great points which bears analogy to truth, and to the doctrines opened to us by divine revelation. I was lately discoursing on this subject with a learned person, who has been very much conversant among the inhabitants of the more western parts of Africa. Upon his conver-

sing

sing with several in that country, he tells me that their notion of heaven, or of a future state of happiness is this, that every thing we there wish for will immediately present itself to us. We find, say they, our souls are of such a nature that they require variety, and are not capable of being always delighted with the same objects. The supreme Being, therefore, in compliance with this taste of happiness which he has planted in the soul of man, will raise up, from time to time, say they, every gratification which it is in the humour to be pleased with. If we wish to be in groves or bowers, among running streams or falls of water, we shall immediately find ourselves in the midst of such a scene as we desire. If we would be entertained with music and the melody of sounds, the concert arises upon our wish, and the whole region about us is filled with harmony. In short, every desire will be followed by fruition, and whatever a man's inclination directs him to, will be present with him. Nor
is

is it material, whether the supreme Power creates, in conformity to our wishes, or whether he only produces such a change in our imagination, as makes us believe ourselves conversant among those scenes which delight us. Our happiness will be the same, whether it proceed from external objects, or from the impressions of the Deity upon our own private fancies. This is the account which I have received from my learned friend. Notwithstanding this system of belief be in general very chimerical and visionary, there is something sublime in its manner of considering the influence of a divine Being on a human soul. It has also, like most other opinions of the heathen world upon these important points; it has, I say, its foundation in truth, as it supposes the souls of good men after this life to be in a state of perfect happiness; that in this state there will be no barren hopes, nor fruitless wishes, and that we shall enjoy every thing we can desire. But the particular circumstance which I am most pleased

pleased with in this scheme, and which arises from a just reflection upon human nature, is that variety of pleasures which it supposes the souls of good men will be possessed of in another world. This I think highly probable, from the dictates both of reason and revelation. The soul consists of many faculties, as the understanding and the will, with all the senses both outward and inward; or, to speak more philosophically, the soul can exert herself in many different ways of action. She can understand, will, imagine, see, and hear, love and discourse, and apply herself to many other the like exercises of different kinds and natures; but what is more to be considered, the soul is capable of receiving a most exquisite pleasure and satisfaction from the exercise of any of these its powers, when they are gratified with their proper objects: she can be entirely happy by the satisfaction of the memory, the sight, the hearing, or any other mode of perception. Every faculty is as a distinct taste in the mind, and hath objects accommodated to its proper relish

R         Dr.

Dr. Tillotson somewhere says, that he will not presume to determine in what consists the happiness of the blessed, because God Almighty is capable of making the soul happy by ten thousand different ways. Besides those several avenues to pleasure which the soul is endued with in this life, it is not impossible, according to the opinions of many eminent divines, but there may be new faculties in the souls of good men made perfect, as well as new senses in their glorified bodies. This we are sure of, that there will be new objects offered to all those faculties which are essential to us.

We are likewise to take notice, that every particular faculty is capable of being employed on a very great variety of objects. The understanding, for example, may be happy in the contemplation of moral, natural, mathematical, and other kinds of truth. The memory likewise may turn itself to an infinite multitude of objects, especially when the soul shall have passed through the space of many millions of
years,

years, and shall reflect with pleasure on the days of eternity. Every other faculty may be confidered in the same extent.

We cannot question but that the happiness of a soul will be adequate to its nature, and that it is not endued with any faculties which are to lye useless and unemployed. The happiness is to be the happiness of the whole man, and we may easily conceive to ourselves the happiness of the soul, while any one of its faculties is in the fruition of its chief good. The happiness may be of a more exalted nature in proportion as the faculty employed is so; but as the whole soul acts in the exertion of any of its particular powers, the whole soul is happy in the pleasure which arises from any of its particular acts. For notwithstanding, as has been before hinted, and as it has been taken notice of by one of the greatest modern philosophers, we divide the soul into several powers and faculties, there is no such division in the soul itself, since it is the whole soul that remembers, under-
stands,

stands, wills, or imagines. Our manner of considering the memory, understanding, will, imagination, and the like faculties, is for the better enabling us to express ourselves in such abstracted subjects of speculation, not that there is any such division in the soul itself.

Seeing then that the soul has many different faculties, or in other words, many different ways of acting; that it can be intensely pleased, or made happy by all these different faculties or ways of acting; that it may be endued with several latent faculties, which it is not at present in a condition to exert; that we cannot believe the soul is endued with any faculty which is of no use to it; that whenever any one of these faculties is transcendently pleased, the soul is in a state of happiness; and in the last place, considering that the happiness of another world is to be the happiness of the whole man; who can question but that there is an infinite variety in those pleasures we are speaking of; and that this fulness

ness of joy will be made up of all those pleasures which the nature of the soul is capable of receiving?

We shall be the more confirmed in this doctrine, if we observe the nature of variety, with regard to the mind of man. The soul does not care to be always in the same bent. The faculties relieve one another by turns, and receive an additional pleasure from the novelty of those objects about which they are conversant.

Revelation likewise very much confirms this notion, under the different views which it gives us of our future happiness. In the description of the throne of God, it represents to us all those objects which are able to gratify the senses and imagination: in very many places it intimates to us all the happiness which the understanding can possibly receive in that state, where all things shall be revealed to us, and we shall know even as we are known; the raptures of devotion, of divine love, the pleasure of conversing with our blessed Saviour, with an innumerable host of Angels, and with the spirits of just men made perfect, are likewise revealed to us in several parts of the holy writings. There are also mentioned those hierarchies of governments, in which the blessed shall be ranged one above another, and in which we may be sure a great part of our happiness will likewise consist; for it will not be there as in this world, where every one is aiming at power and superiority; but on the contrary, every one will find that station the most proper for him in which he is placed, and will probably think that he could not have been so happy in any other station. These and many other particulars are marked in divine revelation, as the several ingredients of our happiness in heaven, which all imply such a variety of joys, and such a gratification of the soul in all its different faculties, as I have been here mentioning.

Some of the Rabbins tell us, that the cherubims are a set of angels who know most,

most, and the seraphims a set of angels who love most. Whether this distinction be not altogether imaginary, I shall not here examine; but it is highly probable, that among the spirits of good men, there may be some who will be more pleased with employment of one faculty than of another, and this perhaps, according to those innocent and virtuous habits or inclinations which have here taken the deepest root.

I might here apply this consideration to the spirits of wicked men, with relation to the pain which they shall suffer in every one of their faculties, and the respective miseries which shall be appropriated to each faculty in particular. But leaving this to the reflection of my readers, I shall conclude, with observing how we ought to be thankful to our great Creator, and rejoice in the Being which he has bestowed upon us, for having made the soul susceptible of pleasure by so many different ways. We see by what a variety of passages joy and gladness may enter into the thoughts of man;

man; how wonderfully a human spirit is framed, to imbibe its proper satisfactions, and taste the goodness of its Creator. We may therefore look into ourselves with rapture and amazement, and cannot sufficiently express our gratitude to him, who has encompassed us with such a profusion of blessings, and opened in us so many capacities of enjoying them.

There cannot be a stronger argument that God has designed us for a state of future happiness, and for that heaven which he has revealed to us, than that he has thus naturally qualified the soul for it, and made it a being capable of receiving so much bliss. He would never have made such faculties in vain, and have endued us with powers that were not to be exerted on such objects as are suited to them. It is very manifest, by the inward frame and constitution of our minds, that he has adapted them to an infinite variety of pleasures and gratifications, which are not to be met with

in

in this life. We should therefore at all times take care that we do not disappoint this his gracious purpose and intention towards us, and make those faculties which he formed, as so many qualifications for happiness and rewards, to be the instruments of pain and punishment.

FINIS.

*Books*

*Books lately published by G. KEARSLEY.*

TRAVELLERS in FRANCE, ITALY, SWITZERLAND, and HOLLAND.

To those who intend to visit the Continent, the following Companions are recommended; they are well stored with that sort of Information which every Traveller will find necessary; are but a trifling Expence, and take up very little Room in the Pocket or Portmanteau; each containing an accurate Map, and the latest Regulations relative to Travellers by Post, in the Diligences, by Water, or on Horseback. The Distances of the Towns and Villages from each other, and the best Houses of Accommodation, with an Explanation of the different Coins, and a Description of such Things as are worth a Stranger's Notice, are also accurately inserted.

The TOUR of FRANCE is 3s. 6d.
ITALY 4s. 6d.
HOLLAND 3s. 6d.
SWITZERLAND 2s. 6d.

Any of which may be had separate.

---

The FOURTH EDITION, much enlarged,

(Ornamented with a considerable Number of new Plates, containing several Views in the newly discovered Islands, sundry Animals, an exact Representation of an Human Sacrifice, Captain Cook's Head from Pingo's Medal, and a Chart of the new Discoveries with the Tracks of the Ships)

In Two Volumes,

An accurate ABRIDGEMENT of CAPT. COOK's VOYAGE round the WORLD; containing a faithful Account of all the Discoveries, with the Transactions at each Place, a Description of the Inhabitants with their Manners and Customs, a full Detail of the Circumstances relative to Capt. Cook's Death, and an Account of his Life by Capt. King.

Those

*ooks lately published by G. KEARSLEY.*

Those who superintend the Education of Youth of either Sex cannot put into their Hands a more acceptable Work, for the Amusement of leisure Hours, than these late Voyages of Discovery, which abound with Matter highly interesting and entertaining.

Price Eight Shillings in Boards.

*⁂* Either Volume may be had separate, Price Four Shillings.

---

With five new Plates, from the Designs of Mr. Nixon,
The Tenth Edition of that pleasing Selection,
The BEAUTIES of STERNE.
Calculated for the Heart of Sensibility.

This Volume contains a Selection of Mr. Sterne's Familiar Letters, the Story of Le Fevre and Uncle Toby, Maria, Shandy's Bed of Justice, Yorick's Horse, Corporal Trim's Brother, the Dwarf, the Pulse, the Pye-man, the Sword, the Supper, the Starling, the Ass, Dr. Slop and Obadiah, Dr. Slop and Susan, &c.

Also several of his most celebrated Sermons and elegant Sentiments.

Price Three Shillings and Sixpence sewed.

---

In Four Volumes, Price Twelve Shillings,

The BEAUTIES of the SPECTATOR, TATLER, GUARDIAN, RAMBLER, ADVENTURER, CONNOISEUR, WORLD, and IDLER.

☞ To accommodate the Purchasers of these entertaining Volumes, they are sold together, or in the following manner:

The Selections from the SPECTATOR, TATLER, and GUARDIAN are comprised in the two first Volumes, and sold separate for Six Shillings.

The third and fourth Volumes contain those from the RAMBLER, CONNOISSEUR, ADVENTURER, WORLD, and IDLER, and are sold separate for Six Shillings, or the Four Volumes for Twelve Shillings, complete.

The

*Books lately published by* G. KEARSLEY.

The Eighth Edition corrected,

THE GENTLEMAN's STABLE DIRECTORY; Or MODERN SYSTEM of FARRIERY.

Comprehending the present improved Mode of Practice, containing all the most valuable Prescriptions and approved Remedies, accurately proportioned and properly adapted to every known Disease to which the Horse is incident.

Interspersed with occasional Remarks upon the dangerous and almost obsolete Practice of Gibson, Bracken, Bartlet and others.

Including Directions for Feeding, Bleeding, Purging, and getting into Condition for the Chace.

Inscribed to Sir JOHN LADE, Bart.

By WILLIAM TAPLIN, Surgeon.

†‡† The rapidity of the Sale of Seven Editions of this Book, and the general Enquiry for it since the new Edition has been at Press, may be fairly considered as Proofs of its Merit.

All the Prescriptions are the result of many Years successful Practice.

Price Seven Shillings bound, or Six Shillings in Boards.